The Daly News

SHORT NOTES

The Daly News

by
Joel Daly

Eckhartz Press · Chicago

ECKHARTZ
PRESS

Copyright 2014 by Joel Daly

Published in the United States by Eckhartz Press,
Chicago, Illinois

Cover design by Steve Holodnicki
Interior design by Kelly Hyde

Photos from the personal collection of Joel Daly

All rights reserved

No part of this book may used or reproduced in
any manner without written permission except
in the case of brief quotations embodied in critical
articles or reviews.

ISBN #: 978-0-9894029

Second Edition

Foreword

By Kate Scott Daly

While the city knows Joel Daly, I know "Papa" (my grandfather). I know the man who played harmonica with me and wore slippers on a Sunday afternoon. I know the man who popped popcorn and let me stay up late to watch James Bond movies and listen to Johnny Cash and Willie Nelson. I know the man who cooks steak when I come to visit and clips out interesting articles for me to read.

My mom would turn on the TV at 4 pm when I came home from school, and I would wave at the screen, believing he could see me.

He would bring me to the studio, and I would watch in awe as his voice filled a silent room, delivering the news to hundreds of thousands of people. I felt strength coming from him that I'd never felt before. I think Chicago felt it too.

When I was 7 years old, Papa gave me a scarf to keep me warm in winter. It was his old Yale scarf, something I had always coveted. When he gave it to me, he told me that I could go there when I was older. I never asked questions. I just knew that if he believed I could do it, I could.

"Pa Pa" and Kate

Papa has always been my biggest inspiration. He showed me the beauty of imagination. When I was little, I would go to my grandparents' lake house every weekend, and after Grammy tucked me in, Papa would storm into the room with a stool above his head, proclaiming that there were lions under my bed. Out of the circus, he would turn into a lion tamer, keeping me safe from the vicious beasts. I became a writer because of him.

My grandparents are beautiful. They have been married over 50 years, and through trauma and triumph, they have kept a sense of humor and a stronger bond than anyone could imagine. Both of them have worked hard to provide an amazing future for me. All the long hours he put in, all of the gritting trips overseas. I can only hope I have made him proud.

All my love,

Kate

The Daly News

by
Joel Daly

Chapter 1

"To Be. Or not To Be"

Twenty-six years old, unshaven and sunburned, I was crossing the Mekong River, separating Laos and Thailand, on a real Chinese "Junk." It was a sunny spring time morning in 1961. The Pathet Lao, a communist guerrilla group, was threatening our stalwart ally, Thailand, with invasion. My employer, the Scripps Howard television station in Cleveland, Ohio, had sent me on my first overseas assignment. Armed only with a 16-millimeter film camera and the confidence of youth, I was intent on recording the sights and sounds of the impending crisis.

I came equipped with a Yale diploma, a few years of experience in radio and TV, and a foolhardy abundance of overconfidence. I was still wearing the fatigues and combat boots left over from my nearly three year sojourn as an Army broadcast specialist in the Panama Canal Zone that had ended two years earlier. The patches and stripes had been removed. But one could tell from the stitching that remained that I was an enlisted man, not an officer. That fact raised some curiosity when I made my way north from Bangkok and blundered into the tents of U.S. colonels and majors, at Udorn Air Force Base, seeking directions.

A nice captain, who befriended me during my northerly meanderings, drove me to the river that morning and gave me some old World War Two C-rations for a snack along the way. Suspicious of the local water supply, I had drunk the juice from a can of peaches to stifle my thirst. But that was hours earlier.

I was totally parched when I finally reached the Laotian shore. It was all jungle with a narrow dirt road along the shoreline. And, unbelievably, there was a waiting taxi! I asked the driver to take me to Vientiane, the Laotian capital.

About half way there, I spotted an American soldier, a Green Beret, on guard in the middle of a field. I told the driver to stop and grabbed my camera. Americans were not supposed to be in Laos! I approached the young sergeant and asked if he had any water he could share. He looked disapprovingly at my non-regulation fatigues, slapped his canteen, and announced: "No water allowed until 11-hundred hours." It was only 0-9-hundred. So I started shooting film, as he whispered into a walkie-talkie. Within minutes, a Jeep driven by an angry-looking major arrived. He told me to get in.

I finally got a drink of water. But the major said he would have to take my film as this was a restricted area, and all pictures were off-limits.

Then he proudly showed me weapons his men had taken from the Pathet Lao. I asked him if I could take pictures to show the folks at home. He happily posed, returned my film, and told me to go on my way.

When I reached Vientiane, I had the driver take me to the Continental Hotel, which I knew to be the headquarters for foreign correspondents. They marveled at my arrival, but told me I would be unable to leave without a visa. I had one to get in but not to get out. So, I drove to the U.S. Consul where a native employee explained it would take 48 hours to secure a visa. What could I do? "You might try Colonel 'So and So' at Army Headquarters," he explained. So, I instructed my nervous driver that was where we were going next!

Tired and hot, I sat in the colonel's office beneath a slow-moving ceiling fan. The building was perched on stilts with palm trees hitting the open screens. I felt like I was in an old "jungle movie." The colonel was all "spit and polish" and spoke excellent English. "Where did you go to school?" he asked. I told him. He brightened and said, proudly, "I went to Columbia. I was an English Major..." "So was I," I exclaimed.

And so for the next hour, with the palm trees brushing the open screens beside us and the slow fan moving the humidity above us, we discussed Shakespeare. What a surreal scene! The colonel was particularly interested in *King Lear*. Finally, I looked at my watch and explained I had a reservation on the next flight to Bangkok. Could I make it? "Of course," he said, "I will provide an escort." Now, my driver was really impressed as military motorcycles paved his way, unimpeded, to the airport.

There, I waved jauntily to the correspondents waiting to ship their film; the same ones who told me, at the hotel, I couldn't get out of there for 48 hours. One of them, the AP's Peter Arnett, had advised me it was a waste of time going on to Viet Nam. That was just a little "police action", he explained, that would be over in six months. So instead I went on to Hong Kong and Tokyo, skipping Saigon. Peter later won a Pulitzer Prize for his coverage of the war.

Chapter 2

"Home. Home on the Range…"

Before I received a scholarship to Yale, I had never been east of Great Falls, Montana, where I was born, August 21, 1934. My father, Joseph, a decorated soldier in World War One, married my mother, Viola, after the War, and became a highly successful used-car salesman. But, the Depression closed the car lots and the family moved to Kalispell, where my brother, Dan, was born. Then it was on to Missoula as Dad looked for a better job.

Finally, a great offer: Dad was offered the job of Sales Manager of a Chevrolet dealership in San Francisco. We headed west! We got as far as Idaho when the Japanese bombed Pearl Harbor. My Mom, I later learned, refused to go on to California. That's how we wound up in Spokane, Washington. I was six, at the time, eligible for the first grade. My educational journey had begun, with kindergarten, in a real one-room schoolhouse in the middle of an Idaho potato field where I distinguished myself playing the bird whistle in the Rhythm Band.

I switched to the trumpet in grade school and by the fifth grade had my own band, "Joe Daly and the Hot Shots." We played at assemblies and talent shows and even made a radio appearance. Music sustained and motivated me right through college. Although I played "first chair," I knew I was simply a "mechanic." I could memorize but I couldn't improvise.

With some success as a debater and orator, I opted for the "spoken word." I couldn't afford to go to college, but I read about "radio announcing schools" in California. That's what I would do! But my debate coach, Grace Becher, thought I could do better. She insisted that I apply for college scholarships. Which I did. I even took summer school to complete a second year of Latin to meet the language requirement of most major universities. Yale responded with a full scholarship. My life was about to change!

No one in my family had ever gone to college. Dad worked a number of menial jobs: Kaiser Aluminum, the White Pine Lumber Company, and the Millwood Paper Mill. He ended up as a beloved bartender at the "Mill Tavern," just a few miles from where we lived. Mom worked as an audiologist for a Hearing Aid company in Spokane. My sister, Patrice, was born when I was twelve. A wonderful surprise! I helped to raise her, as Mom suffered several mental breakdowns and had to be institutionalized periodically.

Finally, Uncle Bill and Aunt Pauline, Mom's sister, took Pat with them to their home in Rock Island, Illinois and shipped my brother and me off to relatives in Montana to work on their ranch. I worked for the next three summers for my cousin on his spread near Conrad. That's where I learned to drive, drink an occasional beer, and yodel. The latter talent got me through a number of Yale social functions and served as the foundation for a rewarding avocation as a country and western singer. (More on that later!)

It doesn't rain much in Montana in the summertime. But, when it does it means an afternoon of fun and games. It was on one of those afternoons that I met an older neighbor named Palmer Oleson. Palmer was a real cowboy! He worked on the Alaskan Highway, rode bulls at the rodeo, played guitar, and yodeled. I was enthralled. So, every day, as I drove the noisy, smelly old Oliver tractor in the field, I tried to yodel. Since I couldn't hear myself, I was never discouraged. Then, one day, as I unfastened the equipment, out in the middle of the sod, I tried a "yodel lay hee hoo." And out it came! Wow! I was hooked. I wore cowboy boots the rest of my life.

4311 No. Argonne Rd. "Family Home"

Joel Daly

The Daly's

Joel's 60th Birthday

Chapter 3

"...Lux et Veritas..."

The outfit I wore to Yale after a three-day train trip to New Haven, in the fall of 1952, was less "Old Prairie" and more like "New California"—a maroon sport coat with puckered lapels and huge shoulder pads. My hair was long and slicked back in a stylish "duck's ass." How out of place, was I, among the crew cut, white-bucked prep school lads. I held out for a year before I gave in to the campus fashion. I even started smoking a pipe!

My first night in the dorm set the tone for the "bright college years" to follow. As I sat, unsettled and lonely, in my third floor dorm room in Wright Hall, the door opened on the first-floor landing and the Whiffenpoofs sang their songs:

"To the Tables down at Mory's...to the place where Louie dwells..."

I never met "Louie," but I met and made wonderful, lifetime friends in the then all-boys school. My second year, I was assigned to Jonathon Edwards College. Paul Kerrigan and Hugo Guidotti were my roommates who greeted me every time I returned from class with a chorus of "It's Howdy Doody Time." Something about the freckles and big ears! The following years, I roomed with Bob Garlock, Roger Englander and Don Chatfield. We adapted a stray cat we named "Dido." Dido and I never got along. She liked to leave "presents" under my bed. But when she gave birth to a litter of kittens, my roomies were away for the weekend. I acted as "midwife."

As a scholarship student, I had to work a bursary job. I was assigned to the Art Library. To stay in school, I had to maintain a certain grade average. The young man, who preceded me from Spokane, the year before, flunked out, so the pressure was even greater. I excelled in—of all things—chemistry! But English Literature was my forte. Philosophy became a second major.

During a "Logic" exam, I literally spilled blood on my blue book. Suffering from a terrible head cold, I developed a nosebleed. To finish the test, I sat upright, my head back, writing without looking or thinking. I figured I had failed; and later asked the instructor if I could do some make-up work. Didn't matter—I got an A. That taught me one thing about logic. Don't think too much!

Building on my high school talents, I joined the Band and the Debating Society and my sophomore year, I "heeled" or competed to become a member of the campus radio station, WYBC. That was my entrée to broadcasting. Eventually, as Chief Announcer, I interviewed campus guests from Frank Lloyd Wright to Jayne Mansfield. I met Julie Andrews, who was 18, when she opened in New Haven in "My Fair Lady." It was heady stuff for this kid from Spokane.

One of the highlights of my debating experience was the "Humorous Debate" against Princeton. The issue was: "Resolved the Dior Look Falls Flat." That was the year Dior de-emphasized the bosom and we took the side of feminine modesty, replete with Boy Scout uniforms and a pitcher of milk at the table.

One of the memorable social events—and there weren't many for a scholarship student on a very limited budget—was a "Roman Orgy" at J.E. It was a toga party, and the only time we were allowed in the dining room without a coat and tie. I added an epee from the Fencing

Team to my costume. Not a good idea, as it turned out. One of our professors, the brilliant Art Historian, Vincent Scully—himself, an old fencer—challenged me to a duel. He wound up falling and breaking his wrist. But, he refused to divulge the identity of his assailant and I escaped severe disciplinary action.

During spring and Christmas vacations the time was too short and the distance too great to return to Spokane, so I hitched a ride to Rock Island, Illinois and stayed with my Aunt and Uncle. During the Christmas break, junior year, I visited WHBF and applied for a "summer replacement" job. I later received an offer. And I had to make a tough decision.

To maintain a student deferment during the Korean War, I had to become a member of the ROTC. I opted for the Air Force and was deemed "pilot qualified." As my third year came to an end, I had to choose between summer camp—and an eventual commission, and pilot's wings, in the Air Force—or the Rock Island job. I chose the latter and my life's course was set. Much later I would learn to fly.

Kid From Spokane Class of 1956

Roman Orgy

WYBC

Chapter 4

"*Summertime, and the Livin' is Easy...*"

"The Summer of '55." If it wasn't a movie title, it should have been! For the first time, I was working in television. I filled in for regular staffers on vacation: everything from a man-on-the street program to a children's show. The Farmer's Noontime Report was a highlight—news about the "price of hogs."

I auditioned for the Quad Cities Music Guild and landed a part in *Of Thee I Sing*. My Uncle Bill helped me buy a used car, a 1949 Chevrolet Coupe. I had wheels but few deals. Dating was difficult because I never knew from week to week what days I would have off. One day I was browsing in McCabe's Department Store, a block from the station, and saw a young lady buying white hose for her upcoming nurses training. I knew the clerk, so I sauntered over to say hello.

I was wearing Bermuda shorts with long black sox, then an oddity in Middle America. The young lady looked at me and asked: "What happened to your pants?" I liked her attitude, so I watched her sign her name and address to the charge account: "Sue Weis" (my first success as an investigative journalist). Later, I called and we started dating. Mostly to church affairs. Her Dad was a doll. He liked me and cooked steaks and introduced me to good Scotch. Later, he told his daughter, "That's the man you're going to marry." He was right!

The summer went too fast. It was back to school for my final year. I parlayed my summertime experience into a weekend gig on a local

New Haven radio station, WAVZ. I spun records and read the hourly news, "Your old D.J...J.D." One of my colleagues, a little man, with a big voice, extolled his experience as an Army broadcaster. It got him to New York. Wow—sounded like a plan! My student deferment, at the draft board, would end after graduation, so I decided to enlist for three years to ensure my assignment as a broadcast specialist. But, first graduation, and receipt of a diploma written in Latin, inscribed *magna cum laude*.

> **PRAESES ET SOCII**
> **UNIVERSITATIS YALENSIS**
> IN NOVO PORTU IN RE PUBLICA CONNECTICUTENSI OMNIBUS AD QUOS HAE LITTERAE PERVENERINT SALUTEM IN DOMINO SEMPITERNAM NOS PRAESES ET SOCII HUIUS UNIVERSITATIS
> *Joel Thomas Daly*
> PRIMI HONORIS ACADEMICI CANDIDATUM AD GRADUM TITULUMQUE ARTIUM LIBERALIUM BACCALAUREI ADMISIMUS EIQUE CONCESSIMUS OMNIA IURA PRIVILEGIA INSIGNIA AD HUNC HONOREM SPECTANTIA IN CUIUS REI TESTIMONIUM HIS LITTERIS UNIVERSITATIS SIGILLO IMPRESSIS NOS PRAESES ET SCRIBA ACADEMICUS SUBSCRIPSIMUS a.d. III ID. IUN. ANNO DOMINI MDCCCCLVI ET UNIVERSITATIS YALENSIS CCLV
>
> *Gradus delatus magna cum laude*
>
> SCRIBA   PRAESES

Chapter 5

"You're in the Army now..."

It was mid-July, when I boarded the bus for Fort Dix, New Jersey. Eight weeks of basic training where all the veneer of Yale was peeled away with dull work and dirty duties. One day, while performing sit-ups on the drill field, I watched planes taking off from nearby McGuire Air Force Base and wondered if I had made a mistake to leave the Air Force! But, finally, it was over and the Army kept its promise. I was sent to Broadcast School at Fort Slocum in New Rochelle, New York.

But then the guarantees were ignored. Those in the top of the class were promised their choice of assignments. I wanted to go to Germany, home of the revered Armed Forces Network. I studied conversational German in college and spoke it rather fluently. I was third in my class, but was sent, instead, to Fort Eustis, Virginia, the Army Transportation Center, a school for truck drivers!

There was no broadcast work available so I was assigned as a clerk typist at the base hospital, where I had plenty of time to read Army regulations. It was the start of my legal education. I knew my rights and exercised them. I even drove to the Pentagon a couple of times. Exasperated, the Army finally assigned me to the Signal Corps at Fort Lee, New Jersey. I was only there a week, when I swapped orders with a young family man, who was being transferred to the Panama Canal Zone. Off to the tropics!

Chapter 6

"Carnival..."

The Canal Zone was a 60-mile strip of American colonialism. It had its own police force, post office, and commissary. The residents were smug, civil service employees of the Pan Canal Company. Panamanians were primarily domestics and laborers who had to be out of "Little America" at dusk. Entrenched in the middle and at both ends of the Zone were military bases: Army, Navy and Air Force.

CFN—the Caribbean Forces Network—was located at Fort Clayton, near Balboa, on the Pacific side of the Canal. At the time, it boasted the only television station in Central America... thus a national showcase. For me, it was an oasis of opportunity. Ultimately, I produced a morning radio show and the 6:00 pm television news.

Before leaving the States, I proposed to Sue by letter—very businesslike! I was a lowly private making $76.00 a month. But, I explained her dependent's allotment would nearly double that. She was only 19 and welcomed what would become a two-year honeymoon.

Without enough rank to qualify for base housing, I found "vacation housing" in the Canal Zone. Pan Canal employees would take lengthy vacations and would rent their houses to young couples to keep it free from mildew and retain their maid. In all, we moved seven times in two years, with the aid of a 1946 Nash Ambassador I bought for $400.00. It was great transportation but had trouble negotiating the hills because of a faulty fuel injector. But it coasted great!

After our marriage in Rock Island, August 24, 1957 and a two-day honeymoon at Starved Rock State Park, the newly-weds finally settled in Balboa. We shared a home with another military couple, playing Scrabble in the evening and watching movies on Friday night at the Air Force Base for 50 cents a couple. The night would often end at the Curundu Commissary with a lively game of charades. It was simple, but it was fun!

Eventually, Sue got a job in the gift shop of the local YMCA, which qualified us for our own quarters. It was a one-bedroom duplex...a screened-in box. Mary Reese, Sue's co-worker, and her husband, Will, an Army baker, occupied the other side. We were great friends and we had great times. The Army was generous with recreational activities and we went deep-sea fishing, swimming, and made excursions into the jungle and along the Canal. I celebrated my last New Year's Day by spitting in both oceans and peeing in the Canal.

The Daly News

My broadcast schedule amounted to a split-shift: radio in the morning, television in the evening. From 6:00 to 10:00, I played records and invited members of the armed forces to "live gaily with Daly." I developed several alter-ego characters most notably, "Sam Sturdley." I, literally, never knew what "he" was going to say. It was kind of scary!

Producing a 15-minute newscast each night was equally creative. I used wire photos from the Associated Press and Signal Corps film to provide generic visuals, along with tape reports from Armed Forces Radio in New York. Occasionally I would get local film of military exercises or "parades."

One of the big stories involved an abortive invasion of Panama by a group of Cubans, following Castro's coup, New Year's Day of 1959. They came ashore on the Atlantic side and promptly got lost in the jungle. National correspondents flew in for the folly. I made several reports for the "Today Show." It was heady stuff!

It was about this time that I changed my name from "Joe" to "Joel," my real name. Mom wanted her firstborn to be a "Joe," like Dad, but not a "Junior." She found the name "Joel" in the Old Testament, a minor prophet no one had ever heard of. I hated the name! Which is why Jim Pattison, the civilian program director—to bug me—always used the formal name in introducing me on any number of panel shows. Eventually, I began to like how it sounded and kept it.

In addition to discussion shows, I also fronted the annual United Fund Telethon, which featured talent from both Panama and the Canal Zone. I interviewed a number of guests, visiting Panama, including Woody Herman and his "Third Herd," actor Raymond Massey, and the inspirational evangelist, Billy Graham. Miss World also dazzled the troops!

Obviously, my enlistment gamble paid off. The Panama experience prepared me for the real world. Toward the end of my term, Sue was pregnant with our first child and left early for home. Back in the barracks, I saw a way to follow her. I entered the Army Entertainment Contest—as a comedian—and got an early release to compete in the Finals, at Fort Belvoir, Virginia. I got a tailored dress uniform out of the deal and a march-on appearance with everyone else on the "Ed Sullivan Show."

My final stop was back at Fort Dix. But now, I had three stripes. No more calisthenics. I left the gate, with my Discharge Papers, as Dinah Washington was singing on the radio, "What a Difference a Day Makes."

My Bride

"Live Gaily......with Daly"

Joel Daly

In The Field

The Daly News

THE ARGUS ROUNDUP, SATURDAY, FEBRUARY 8, 1958

Channel Chatter
By Charles H. Sanders

Yawn Patrol

A former WHBF summertime announcer now is one of the most popular early morning deejays in the entire country of Panama.

He is Joel Daly, a private first class stationed in the Central American country with the Army. Daly is the nephew of Mr. and Mrs. W. C. Goldschmidt, 2010 21st St., Rock Island. His wife, the former Suzon Kay Weis, who also is in Panama City, is the daughter of Mr. and Mrs. Victor Louis Weis, 4024 28th Ave., Rock Island.

The 23-year-old has wowed them in the narrow nation of Panama, both military and civilian residents alike, according to a feature story which appeared recently in two English language newspapers there — the Panama Star & Herald and the Panama American.

Each weekday morning, military personnel and civilians gather their early wits about them with the help of the amiable CFN disk jockey and his "friends" on Yawn Patrol to start the day "living gaily with Daly," according to the articles.

The radio public continues living gaily with a weekly afternoon Pop Shop and on weekends with Saturday Date for Saturday Evening, both programed by Daly.

Fictional 'Friends'

Gathered about him on his programs are his "friends," the most varied group of characters ever assembled under one roof and all figments of his imagination and voice characterizations:

Daly isn't a native of Rock Island, but of Spokane, Wash. However he has spent several summers here with his uncle and aunt during which time

JOEL DALY

he met his wife. They were married last August.

It was during the summer of 1955 that Daly worked at WHBF, both radio and television. He served as relief announcer while regulars were on vacation. He also appeared as Officer Clancy on Milt Boyd's afternoon television series, Grandpa Happy.

Also that summer he took an active part in the Quad-City Music Guild. He played one of the politicians in the Guild's production of "Of Thee I Sing." In addition, he made the tape recordings which were used off stage as a part of the Gershwin musical.

Seeks TV Career

Daly, a magna cum laude graduate of Yale University, plans to enter radio and television as a career after his release from the Army in the summer of 1959.

Besides his radio experience in Rock Island, Daly was chief announcer at Yale's campus station, WYBC, when he was a student majoring in English. In addition, he worked one summer at a radio station in Coeur d'Alene, Idaho, several miles from his home in Spokane, and also on WAVZ in New Haven, Conn.

While at Yale, he interviewed personalities on various network radio shows, such as NBC's Monitor and appeared on Walter Cronkite's CBS show in a filmed humorous debate. An article on Daly appeared recently in Deejay, the national disk jockey magazine.

Pfc. Daly, the son of the late Joseph Daly and Mrs. Daly of Spokane, was assigned to the Army's Caribbean command in April of 1957. He returned to Rock Island for his wedding last Aug. 24 in Immanuel Lutheran Church.

Chapter 7

"Go West Young Man..."

I arrived in Cleveland, before it became "the mistake on the lake" with a flip of a coin. I stopped in Pittsburgh, while dropping audition tapes along the way, and had to decide: north or south: Cleveland or Cincinnati? The coin said "Cleveland"! The Greyhound headed north and west. Armed with addresses taken from the Yellow Pages, at the "Y" where I was staying, I made the rounds of local radio stations. WGAR, the flagship CBS station, atop the Hilton Hotel, just happened to be looking for an announcer. I auditioned and got the job—one week out of the Army! I went on to Rock Island to meet my new son, Douglas.

A week later we headed for Cleveland in a 1959 Plymouth that Sue's Dad helped us buy. We had our kid in a crib and our Panamanian parrot, Boop, in a cage on the back seat. We had to leave the windows open because the car had no air conditioning. It was a hundred degrees when we went through Chicago. We towed a trailer full of hand-me-down furniture and arrived at Shaker Square and our first apartment.

Life was good. I made $400 a month. The rent was $120. The "Rapid" was a block from the apartment and took me right into downtown Cleveland for my early-morning newscasts. On weekends, I hosted a show of Barbershop Quartets and conducted celebrity interviews with guests staying at the Hilton. I was at WGAR less than a year when I got a call from Bill Beutel, whom I had replaced when he went to a local television station, WEWS. He was headed for New York and suggested I try for the TV job. That dusty trail which began in Montana got a little wider.

The WEWS newsroom, which sent me to Southeast Asia a year later, employed me, primarily, as a reporter-cameraman. I enjoyed the film work. The station outfitted my blue-finned Plymouth with a police scanner and a phone and I covered every fire and fender-bender in the city. I always came home smelling like soot! Our second son, Scott, was born, and we moved into larger quarters.

In addition to the roving reporter role, I also wrote a 15-minute newscast for Tom Field, the station's avuncular news-reader. I poured all of my talents as an English Major into his shows. As I filed the scripts, each evening, I envisioned they would be discovered someday and admired for their literary brilliance.

Occasionally, I got to report, on-air, about two-and-and-a-half minutes of local news and on weekends I had my own news program. One Labor Day I was so proud to have filmed a number of local events, processing and editing the film, and writing the script. Unfortunately, I left the film on the editing table and all I had, in the studio, was a bunch of narration with no pictures.

WEWS was the local ABC affiliate and I reported some stories of national interest for the network news. The Civil Rights movement was underway and violent riots broke out on the city's east side. It was my first time under fire. The first national casualty was a white Lutheran Minister, run over by a bulldozer at a disputed school construction site. Dr. Martin Luther King, Jr. came to Cleveland, trying to calm his followers. His visit provided one of my most unforgettable interviews. He spoke in the familiar cadence of parallel phrases: "You can't be what you want to be until I can be what I want to be". "We will either live together as brothers or perish together as fools."

King was a frequent visitor to Cleveland during the '60's raising funds for organizations such as the Southern Christian Leadership Conference. He urged voter registration and participation; and bolstered the local non-violent civil rights movement. He also actively supported the candidacy of Carl Stokes who became America's first big-city black mayor.

Another Cleveland visitor during these turbulent days was Alabama Governor George Wallace, who stood in the schoolhouse door to prevent the integration of the University of Alabama. His message was the familiar "Segregation now. Segregation forever." But, the most memorable part of his visit was his entourage. A small contingent of Alabama State Troopers preceded the Governor into our studio overturning waste baskets and peering behind the curtains to make sure there was no threat.

In the 1972 Presidential campaign, Wallace was paralyzed in an assassination attempt. He later recanted his racist views and asked for the forgiveness of black Americans.

A less hostile crowd greeted The Beatles on their first national tour. It was September 15, 1964. I went to Public Square after the 11:00 News, to watch the screaming crowd, awaiting the group's arrival at the Sheraton Cleveland Hotel. Somehow another reporter and I got swept up by the security detail guarding the rear entrance, and wound up in the Beatles' suite. I spent most of the night in casual conversation with the Fab Four. I didn't realize until years later what a big deal it was!

The Beatles were on the last stop of a month-long tour and were bone-tired. Acknowledging the "groupies" who besieged them everywhere they went, Ringo complained:

"My 'peter' hurts". While I was there an 11-year old girl arrived with a stolen key for a room; a young boy hid in a packing case being delivered; another tried to get into the Kon Tiki bar, pretending to have a reservation; and another pretended to faint outside, only to request that she be given first aid inside the hotel.

The police asked that the Beatles to stay on the same floor where the press conference was held, rather than the Presidential suite, to throw fans off the scent. The press conference provided little 'news'. The Beatles were fidgety, twisting the microphone cords and lighting cigarettes. Someone asked John Lennon: "How did you find America?" He replied "We turned left at Greenland." It was downhill from there: "How many rings does Ringo wear?" "When was your last haircut?" "Don't you trust American barbers?"

Later, the Beatles were spirited by the police to the Public Auditorium for their show. During the third song: "All My Loving", about a hundred fans stormed the stage. Police stopped the show and forced the Beatles to take refuge in their trailer. When peace was restored, it became a "Long Day's Night."

But, the story, which most defined my Cleveland sojourn, was the agonizing saga of Dr. Sam Sheppard. The Bay Village Osteopath was convicted of killing his wife, Marilyn, on the Fourth of July, 1954. Despite his protests that he was innocent, he was sent to prison for life. His description of the alleged intruder—a shaggy-haired man—became the basis for the "one-armed assailant" sought in *The Fugitive* television series many years later.

Everyone in Cleveland had an opinion about Dr. Sam's guilt or innocence. It spurred more arguments than politics or religion. Ten years later, while I was covering the Republican Nominating Convention at the Cow Palace in San Francisco, I got word that the Sixth

Circuit Court of Appeals had granted his petition for *habeas corpus*. It was a bigger story, in Cleveland, than Barry Goldwater's nomination.

I heard the State's appeal before the Supreme Court—my first visit to that hallowed temple of law. Sam's attorney was F. Lee Bailey, a feisty warrior, just three years out of law school. He was brilliant! Bailey happened to attend a cocktail party in New York and overheard Dorothy Killgallen, a syndicated columnist, describe her coverage of the original trial. The Presiding Judge confided to her, in Chambers, "He's guilty as hell!" The Judge's conduct of the trial, which the High Court described as a "circus" earned the defendant a new trial and set the precedent for media coverage in all future trials. Sam was released from prison prior to a new hearing. He had just married a German heiress, Ariane Tebbenjohans—a long-time prison pen pal. The two were wary of all the media attention but welcomed my company and counsel. We became good friends. The more I got to know Sam, the more convinced I was of his innocence. Much later he would be exonerated with the investigation of a former handyman who had worked at the Sheppard home.

But, first there was the re-trial. Many of the original witnesses were now dead; memories had faded. But through his skillful cross-examination, Bailey made it clear to the jury that Sam had been railroaded into a conviction, particularly by the editorial ravings of the Cleveland Press and its editor, Louis Selzer, and the duplicitous testimony of the County Coroner, Sam Gerber. Not Guilty! That was the first time I thought I would like to become a trial lawyer.

Sue and I had Sam and Ariane to our home, one Sunday, for cocktails, to talk about a book. Suddenly, water started pouring through the ceiling. Our daughter, Kelly, who was about two years old, had stopped up the toilet. Sam got right on his knees to wipe up the water. "This is what they taught me in prison," he explained, "I'm used to this." Despite his freedom, Sam never really survived his long incarceration. Sued several times for malpractice, he ultimately lost the medical license restored to him. He divorced Ariane, tried to become a professional wrestler, and died an alcoholic.

Over the years, several of my Cleveland colleagues went to New York and network fame: Bill Beutel, Roger Sharpe, and Jack Perkins. That was also my goal. Ultimately, I received an inquiry from the General Manager of WABC. He talked to my former WGAR News Director, Norm Wagy, who now was an executive at Cleveland's CBS affiliate, WJW-TV. Norm was in the General Manager's office when he took the phone call and extolled my virtues. The General Manager, Bob Buchanan, said: "Hey, if this kid's so good why don't we hire him?" And he did!

At WJW, I was paired with the station's popular anchor, Doug Adair. We became the first in-studio anchor-team in the country. Norm simply said, "Do what you want" and we did. Until this time, the newscast was separated by specific segments: News, Weather, and Sports. Each segment was sponsored individually and separated by commercials. We put the commercials in the middle of the segment so we could, for example, throw it to the weatherman; and he could pass it off to the sportscaster. In that manner, we became more of a 'family'. We had to break down some barriers both with the Sales Department and the Union; but we prevailed.

Because of our great friendship and respect for one another, Doug and I developed a "sibling-like chemistry" that attracted the viewers. We became very successful. The station hired consultants McHugh and Hoffman to maintain and monitor our progress. They exported our success around the country. The format set a pattern for local "eyewitness" news teams in virtually every major city.

In Chicago, the then General Manager of WLS, the ABC owned-and-operated television station, Dick O'Leary, saw one of our tapes. "Let's hire these guys," he decided. Doug and I were both under contract to Storer Broadcasting. I wanted to go; Doug didn't. And, that's how it finally worked out. O'Leary lugged a heavy videotape of our show to New York to show his bosses whom he had hired. They all stood around the tape room commenting how much they liked the anchor with the silver sideburns. "No," said O'Leary, "I hired the other one—the one with the big ears!"

The Daly News

R, SUNDAY, SEPTEMBER 6, 1964   19—E

And Their Ratings Keep Climbing

Ace Newsmen Daly and Adair Mark Banner Year on Channel 8

By Bert J. Reesing
Television-Radio Editor

When two dynamic personalities who are professional mikemen with a rich background of knowhow get together, it's almost a certainty that their news program will be paralleled on one side by sincerity and legitimate news reporting and on the other by success in the field.

Such is the case with Joel Daly and Doug Adair of WJW-TV, Channel 8, who tomorrow mark the first anniversary of their newscasting in double harness on the 11 p.m. "Channel 8 Reports" program.

The news show which started last Sept. 7, has enjoyed snowballing acceptance from the viewing public.

Although the team started out last fall with the station at the bottom of the local news ladder, the two-man gang has become recognized as a leader in newscasting in the unprecedented time of one year. At the time of their premiere program they were pitted against Bill Jorgenson at KYW in the 11 p.m. news slot and controversial Jorgenson had the local screens pretty much to himself.

The WJW ratings, however, continued to climb dispite Jorgenson's early foot on the scene and also because of the WJW non-editorializing of news. Editorializing of the news seemed to have become a habit... an irritating habit to many viewers.

Today, the Daly-Adair team enjoys a Monday-through-Friday rating average which puts them close to the top in local competition. The latest American Research Bureau (ARB) ratings classify Cleveland-11 p.m. news shows (five-day average) as follows:

KYW-TV, 18; WJW-TV, 16; WEWS, 11.

But on Thursday evenings, when the news show breaks into the movie, the ratings show Channel 8 on top with a rating of 20, followed by Channel 3 with 18, and Channel 5 with 9.

The Daly-Adair team is the dark-horse entry in the newscasting field a formidable contender in just one year.

Both Daly and Adair have seperate news shows earlier each evening. Doug Adair presents "City Camera" as part of the 6 p.m. "Channel 8 Report" and Daly has been doing "Cleveland Scene" on the same program.

Adair, an Episcopalian, also serves his faith as well as a lay minister delivering more than 30 sermons a year. He is seen on Channel 8 every Sunday morning at 10:30 on "Moral View" in which he presides as moderator with two or more ministers as guests.

TV On the Air — Radio

Does this affect in any way his role as a hardnews reporter and newscaster? As Adair puts it, "A newscaster can easily be a source of good or evil simply by the way he plays his stories. Ratings can rise if you say something derogatory about someone but I think that's the hard way to go."

The newscaster feels God is looking over his shoulder at his scripts. "God is my Silent News Editor," he says.

A graduate of Northwestern University with a TV-Radio major, Adair often is called upon to host WJW-TV Specials. Doug and his wife, the former Mary Janice Fudge, and their children Lee, Tim and Lynn reside in Brecksville.

Daly, with a background of a magna cum laude graduation from Yale and a stint in the Army as news director and chief announcer for the Carribean Forces Network, adds much to the articulate and concise pattern of the program. He and his wife, Suzon, and sons, Doug and Scott, live in Parma Heights.

The station's profile on the two lists Adair's pet project as the Sunday morning telecast of "Moral View"; it discloses that Daly's leisure time is devoted to photography, sports cars, music, and fiction writing.

Nowhere, though, does it mention their addiction to the pipe. You can see them any day on upper Euclid Avenue with their briars smoking like "Old '97."

Where there's smoke there's fire; and where there's news, you'll find Daly and Adair

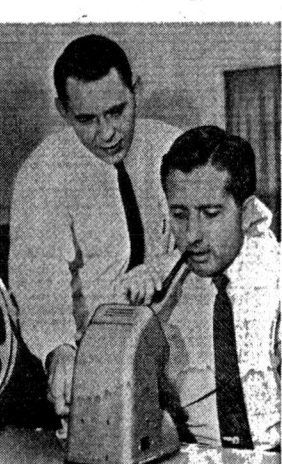

Joel Daly and Doug Adair

News Broadcast

Martin Luther King Jr.

Governor George Wallace

Ariane and Dr. Sam Sheppard

Chapter 8

"Chicago...Chicago...that Toddlin Town..."

We arrived in Chicago in August, 1967. Doug was eight, Scott was six, and Kelly was four. We moved into a grand Victorian-style home on the main street of LaGrange. It was later confirmed to be an early creation of Frank Lloyd

La Grange Home

Wright, built in 1892 for a Civil War General. The third floor ballroom quickly became the kid's play room, and the Tiffany stained-glass windows and marble fireplace became part of our legacy of preservation. We were there for 17 years.

I was driving a little MGB sports car at the time, and was terrified by all the trucks pushing me off the expressway on the way to work. The television station was located at State and Lake, in the heart of the Loop. Originally WBKB, for Paramount owners Balaban and Katz, it later reverted to WLS, the original call sign of the first television station in Chicago, owned by Sears— the "World's Largest Store."

On my first day on the job, several junior executives took me to lunch at a popular delicatessen. The Assistant Program Director, Larry Einhorn, said, "This is the last time you can walk in here unnoticed." He was right! If Chicagoans liked you on the air they were faithful fans forever. Well, almost.

To me, Chicago was "the big time". Let's face it, they don't sing songs about Cleveland:

"On State Street, that great street, I just gotta say, they do things they don't do on Broadway."

I would stand during the dinner hour at the entrance of the station, smoking my pipe, and watch the passing parade of exuberant pedestrians—rich, poor, white and black. Next door to our studios was the State Lake Theater, later to be converted into a studio for Oprah. Fritzel's Restaurant, home of Kup's original "Booth Number One", was kitty-corner, if you jaywalked (and everyone in Chicago did!)

Across the street was Elfman's, where you could get the best corn-beef sandwich in town. It was presided over by Joel Elfman, the self-proclaimed "Prince of State Street". Next to Elfman's was the Chicago Theater, where Bob Hope and so many others had performed. Down the block, at State and Randolph, was the famous Marshall Fields Department Store where people met each other, "under the Clock". This was the epicenter of the city.

At Walgreens across the street, we used to broadcast the city's annual New Year's Eve Party. We put a camera on the roof of the building and focus on the throng, in the intersection, below. The temperature was always below zero. My first year on top of the building, 1967, the crowd got overzealous and pushed our on-the-street-reporter, Art Hellyer, through a plate glass window. Art's back was never the same. Like so many other State Street institutions, the New Year's Eve celebration eventually moved uptown.

But, it was an exciting time to be in the center of the city. As I watched the passing parade, you could feel the rumble of the subway underneath the street. The grates that ventilated the tunnel emitted air that was a constant 65 degrees, which made it feel cool in the summer and warm in the winter. Overhead was the screech of the "L" which took you within a block of Wrigley Field or Comiskey Park.

"Bet your bottom dollar, you'll lose the blues in Chicago...Chicago" my new home town.

Our news staff was relatively small, at the time. When Joe Templeton—whom I was hired to replace—left for ABC News, in Washington, I was the only "anchor", in the shop, which meant a 7-day work week. Frank Reynolds had also migrated to the Network, leaving his buddy, Hugh Hill as our primary street reporter. Les Brownlee came to us from the old *Chicago American*, the first Black TV reporter in Chicago. And Shari Blair was the first female. But, we were still years away from either the first black or woman on the anchor desk.

Dick Goldberg, the News Director, had read some of the celebrity obituaries I had written in Cleveland and suggested that I write something personal for the end of each newscast. He believed that was my *forte*. He was right and the nightly Commentary became my trademark for more than a decade.

Politics dominated our local news. Richard J. Daley was finishing his first decade as a "national king-maker", the "last of the big city Mayors". Maybe it was "an Irish thing", but "da Mayor" was a big fan. I had the temerity to tell him he spelled his last name wrong. It always got a chuckle.

Because of our obvious rapport, I was always stationed at the old Bismark Hotel, Democratic Headquarters, on election night, awaiting the Mayor's benediction. The Party had a "bad night" in November, 1972. The office of Cook County State's Attorney was lost to the Republicans. Daley sat upstairs, refusing to come down to the Press Room.

I urged his Press Secretary, Frank Sullivan: "The Mayor's got to come down, We've been waiting all night". Sullivan told his boss: "Joel says you gotta come down". And, he did. It was 2:00 in the morning. Most deadlines had passed, stations were going off the air. And, instead of Q and A, my colleagues stepped back. It became a dialogue—just the Mayor and me: talking of life, set-backs and success.

Originally, I was a single anchor on the 10:00 News. But, Dick O'Leary was still obsessed with the idea of a two-person format. At the end of 1967, he took Sue and me to dinner to announce he had hired Fahey Flynn, a veteran CBS newsreader, with his signature bow tie, to be my partner.

Sue's comment: "An Irish father-son team? It will never work!" It was the only time she was wrong.

Fahey and I began our adventure on February 12, 1968. John Coleman, a creative weatherman and sportscaster, Bill Frink, joined us. Our partnership would last 15 years, until Fahey's death in 1983. The program won an Emmy six months after its inaugural and within two years was the top-rated 10:00 News in Chicago, if not most of the country. Promoted with inventive and funny commercials, the show earned the sobriquet of "Happy Talk." Despite the unfair criticism, everyone was "happily talking" about us. WLS became the most successful; the most emulated local television station in the country. O'Leary was eventually promoted to President of the ABC network.

Fahey began each newscast with a hearty "How do you do, ladies and gentlemen. I'm Fahey Flynn." Turns out Fahey was one of the radio announcers I listened to as a kid on Saturday night, introducing bands at the Aragon ballroom. We were an "Irish father-son team," as Sue perceived. But, our politics were at opposite ends of the spectrum. This was during "Watergate," the Nixon years and the end of the Viet Nam war. But, whenever I said something in a Commentary with which Fahey disagreed, he would only say: "That's very interesting."

John Coleman was a clown, a showman. But, he was also brilliant and was later responsible for starting *The Weather Channel*. His most-remembered "stunt" was vowing to stand on his head if his forecast was wrong. He was wrong, and he did, and it was painful to watch!

Bill Frink was a journeymen sportscaster and somewhat naïve about the show business aspect of television news. It always frustrated Coleman when he'd argue and win a raise and management would automatically give Frink the same amount. We had a number of colorful reporters like the hale and hearty Hugh Hill. Sheri Blair was the first female and Les Brownlee the first African-American reporter on Chicago television news. At one time Bill Fyffe was news director and Geoff Smith our gourmet-on-the-go. And like me, they had been born in Great Falls, Montana. Figure that!

1968 became one of the most dramatic, career-building times of my life. April saw the assassination of Martin Luther King, in Memphis. It spawned the destructive riots in Chicago's Westside ghetto and triggered Mayor Richard J. Daley's infamous "shoot to kill" order. This was the Commentary I delivered that night:

Commentary—April 8, 1968

Our nation was shocked but not surprised. What a sad and sobering commentary.

Martin Luther King seemed to know that he had a destiny with a sudden and senseless death. Those who loved him and those who hated him seemed to know it too. What a sad and sobering commentary.

A man of peace is dead and violence was not his legacy. People spoke today of hope and love. People reacted today to ignorance and despair. What a sad and sobering commentary.

People talking without speaking; people hearing without listening. Flags at half-staff, rifles at high-port. What a sad and sobering commentary.

The United States of America deeply divided. The so-called "Land of the Free," a veritable land of fear.

Someone must listen. Someone must hear this sad and sobering commentary!

That terrible event was followed within days by the killing of Bobby Kennedy. He was shot down just after winning the California Presidential Primary and announcing, "Now, on to Chicago." Chicago was to be the site of the Democratic National Convention, in August. By mid-summer, the City began filling up with Yippies and Hippies and other young people intent on protesting the war in Viet Nam and, if possible, disrupting the convention. Mayor Daley threw down his gauntlet to so-called "outside agitators."

The stage was set for a major confrontation, which erupted in what was described as a "police riot." As a local reporter behind the security lines I saw the story differently than the network observers.

Commentary—August 28, 1968

Chicago has been described as Stalag '68—America's Prague—Gun City, U.S.A.—an armed camp where it requires a badge for a Democratic delegate to go to the bathroom. Where newsmen are beaten. Yippies are gassed. And, where even a celebrity like Hugh Hefner is subject to a billy club on his bunny tail.

Sad to say, all of this has much foundation in fact and to most of the nation Chicago is no longer just considered a subject for song. It's not just a toddlin' town, but a police state.

And, yet, to balance the picture: millions of Chicagoans continue to live as if nothing were different. Sleeping at home instead of Grant Park, they absorb the delightfully pleasant weather with the diffidence of every day routine. No one checks their credentials or disturbs their labors. They carry no placards; they absorb no punches. They are, more likely, annoyed by the familiar odor of exhaust fumes than the pungent scent of tear gas. And, appear more concerned about the start of school, than the end of the convention.

This is not to say most Chicagoans are not aware of the world attention is focused on their town. But, for everyday people, doing every day things, this is no Prague. There are no tanks in the streets; there are no guns at their backs. And, except what they see and hear on television, or read in the paper, things might seem a little dull in Chicago!

Chicago was totally polarized, with a bad case of perceptual selection: People saw what they wanted to see, heard what they wanted to hear. The network honchos came around to read what I was writing, trying to determine if I was some kind of subversive. Fahey was home ill at the time. In the aftermath of the mass arrests, I was standing outside the Hilton Hotel on Michigan Avenue watching the clean up when a large glass ashtray crashed at my feet. It had been dropped from the 18th floor suite of peace candidate, Eugene McCarthy. In the name of "peace," I was nearly killed.

A year later, a trial was held for the alleged leaders of the student rioting: the "Conspiracy 8," soon to become the "Conspiracy 7."

The Daly News

Commentary—October 29, 1969

Although it has been hailed by some as "the most important political trial in the country's history", the Conspiracy 8 trial often comes off as, as one observer put it, like something "out of a Marx Brothers comedy, as scripted by Salvador Dali."

Not only has the court been trying the defendants, the defendants, in turn, have very deliberately been trying the court and all that it represents.

The conflict today reached tragic proportions when the Judge found it necessary to gag and shackle Black Panther, Bobby Seale. Such an extreme reaction will only further inflame critics who insist the government seeks only to silence those who dissent and suppress those who disagree.

Certainly, it's a shameful picture to show the world. A man, presumably innocent until proven guilty, bound and gagged, a spectacle that mocks the very issues of the trial.

And, that perhaps is the point of this defendant's undisciplined, provocative behavior: to make a mockery of the hearing, to challenge, ironically, what has been this country's most important force for protecting and extending basic human rights.

The Supreme Court, just today, moved dramatically and unanimously against school segregation. This was the so-called "Burger Court." Some thought that would make a difference, which proves, again, that personalities and politics ultimately become submerged in our system of justice.

If the conspiracy law is wrong, it will be overruled. If the Judge errs, he will be reversed. The system does work. But one cannot invoke his rights without an equal sense of responsibility. That's as true in the courtroom as it was last year in Grant Park. And, it's really what this trial is all about.

By and large my Commentaries were well-received. Requests for copies were received virtually every day. At the end of the year, the station published a representative collection of the year's most-requested. The commentaries earned two of my five Emmys—one for content; the other for writing. But, not all of the reaction was favorable. I was predictably threatened by the would-be anarchists who were breaking windows, burning cars and planting bombs. To me, they were simply "cowards"!

The Daly News

Commentary—March 8, 1972

Some powder, a fuse and a spark...such are the basics of a bomb. But of what is the bomber made?

Without courage or compassion, without feeling or concern, the bomber is foremost and first...the worst kind of coward!

With his pliers and wires and cheap little clocks, he's a shadow of a man with "little-boy" thoughts.

Playing hide-and-seek with people's lives, he's less likely to be feared than despised.

Some powder, a fuse and a spark...how simple to build a bomb...how difficult to understand the bomber.

He knows not his victims; how many or why. They may be innocent, unsuspecting, but still they may die.

Coward! Coward! Who would kill without cause: shoppers in Belfast; passengers in tourist-class.

Coward! And cursed, that person who would threaten, extort and indiscriminately destroy for money, vainglory, a red glow in the sky.

Sick minds, it's true, feed on headlines, drool at the damage and laugh at the frightened. But, we cannot ignore nor defer the fact that madmen walk our streets; the worst of assassins, paranoid and plotting.

Some powder, a fuse and a spark. These are the basics of a bomb, but of what is the bomber made?

He is hollow, without soul, an empty shell. The bomber is humanity's "dud".

It was particularly tense during the so-called "Days of Rage". The social "establishment" was under siege. Demonstrations were basically an excuse to break some heads and a whole lot of windows. Those I called "cowards" called me with threats. I took them seriously enough to check my car each night: little pieces of tape to determine that the hood had not been opened.

One night, I asked the LaGrange Police to check my house. A threatening caller not only knew where I lived. He knew how many children I had and how old they were. That was scary!

It was a tumultuous time, but some good things were also happening. On a Sunday night in July of '69, my dog, Florence, and I sat transfixed before the television watching the first lunar landing of the Apollo 11 Astronauts. At 2:00 in the morning I wrote the following:

Commentary—July 20, 1969

"...In the beginning, God created the heaven and the earth..."

Today man—His ultimate and most adaptable creation—put the two in perspective. He left his footprints on the powdery surface of the moon: The first act in a new era; the first verse of a new Genesis.

"...And God said, 'Let there be lights in the firmament of the Heaven to divide the day from the night, and let them be for signs and for seasons and for days and years'..."

The days and years of dreaming, of hoping, of wondering and wishing were fulfilled. Time and space intersected in the shadows of a strange machine called "Eagle"; in a strange place called "Tranquility."

"...And God said let us make man in our image, after our own likeness, and let them have dominion over all the earth..."

Apollo 11 with its daring technology, its courageous crew and national prestige did not in a single, brilliant moment, produce Peace on Earth, Good Will toward Men. Man's dominion is still in powerful disarray.

But, by reaching for the planets, man reaches beyond himself; and takes another great stride away from the primeval caves where he first learned fear and the feuding tribes where he first learned war. By conquering space, he conquers himself...

And, in the end, there is another beginning...a new premise...a greater promise.

Man's evolution is no longer predicated on the survival of the fittest, but the survival of the finest.

"...And God saw everything that he had made and behold, it was very good..."

The Apollo 11 Astronauts, Neil Armstrong, Buzz Aldren and Michael Collins, were welcomed to Chicago, August 13th, for a ticker tape parade, as were most of their colleagues, before and after. Chicago wasn't just the "Second City." It was considered the astronauts' "second home." An invitation from Mayor Daley was issued within minutes of their safe "splashdown"!

The space program was a lifetime fascination. One of my favorite assignments as a young reporter, in Ohio, was covering the "homecoming" of Astronaut, John Glenn, in his hometown of New Concord. Glenn was the third man in space and the first to orbit the earth. At the news conference, held in his old high school gymnasium, I asked the boyish hero: "Do you want to go to the moon?" "That's something I haven't thought about," he answered. That was still a dream at that time.

Some years later, at the end of the Apollo program, I reflected on how far we had traveled—literally!

Commentary—February 8, 1974

The problem with being a dreamer is that you tend to close your eyes, and, for me, the space program, which came to an end today, was the "stuff" of which dreams are made.

Forty-one Americans ventured into the black frontier during the past decade, and they all returned. Their achievements were generally measured in technological terms: how far, how fast, how much.

But, I was more fascinated with the human adventure.

For every flight, every mission, including the one that ended today, succeeded only because man was there, still the most flexible, adaptive, non-mechanized creature to come along.

I remember when Neil Armstrong took that "giant step for mankind," when he put his footprints on the moon, I sat up all night trying to find the right words:

"By reaching for the planets," I concluded, "Man reaches beyond himself and takes another giant stride away from the primeval caves, where he first learned fear, and the feuding tribes, where he first learned war. By conquering space, he conquers himself."

But, I was wrong. I was dreaming! The space program was primarily an engineering feat, quickly forgotten, and, in the final phases, almost ignored.

But it's my hunch that, say, 10,000 years from now, it won't be Watergate or the energy crisis that will dominate the history of this era. It will be our achievement in space, man's first tentative steps into the foothills of the Universe.

History? Ten thousand years from now? Perhaps, that, too, is the mark of a dreamer.

If all seemed well in space, earthly problems were many. In 1970, I made my first, of four trips, to Israel: a beautiful, hopeful country which peace passed over.

Commentary—December 2, 1970

One does not become a Middle East expert in 10 days' time, on only one side of the line, so I shouldn't presume to preach what should or could be done. But, after bouncing around on a bus for several hundred miles, attending a dozen briefings and on-site inspections, several impressions have evolved.

Israel will resume the Peace Talks, probably early next year, as the best way to preserve the ceasefire. Moshe Dayan, in his next trip to Washington, is likely to insist on an armistice commission, some practical and workable way to define and secure the truce. The lack of action and delay in announcement in the latest Suez incident suggests some accommodations may already have been reached.

Israel appears willing to relinquish most of the occupied territory, except for such strategic locations as the Golan Heights. Jerusalem is not negotiable. The Holy City will never again be isolated or divided.

Israel resents its role as a big-power pawn. Many Israelis feel they have been unduly and unwisely pressured by the United States and show little affection for Americans.

Of course, this young country hasn't had time to cultivate the social courtesies to which we are accustomed. The Israelis often appear abrasive, impatient and impolite, even inefficient. Israel is a country where the impossible may be routine and the routine impossible. It would appear they can win a war faster than they can deliver a letter.

Israel, in the final analysis, is not a melting pot but a mosaic, a structure of many different pieces, all held together by an irreducible adhesive—the will to survive.

The station also sent me to the Philippines for the POW homecoming at the end of the Vietnam War, an emotional reunion, reminiscent of the Cuban prisoner exchange I witnessed so many Christmases earlier. Peter Arnett also was there. I reminded him of his shortsighted prediction.

Commentary—February 14, 1973

I will always consider myself privileged to have been present at Clark Field in the

Philippines when the first of our POW's were released.

I have never seen newsmen get so emotionally involved in an event, spontaneously waving, cheering, even crying.

And it's right, and it's good that we should feel this way: These courageous, unfortunate men, and their dead and wounded comrades, have had to pay the highest price for this awful war.

The dead, of course, are gone. No amount of prayers or tears can restore them to us. As for the wounded, we will heal their flesh, as best we can.

But, many also suffer wounds deep in the heart—wounds that are beyond all our skills and arts to heal.

And they will come to know more wounds, and more deaths when they return to pick up the thread of their lives. They will find that the world has moved on. They and their wives have changed. Their children may not even know them anymore. Their friends may try to be too kind to them; their parents too solicitous.

At a war's end, we can mark the graves of the dead, and cover the scars of the wounded. But, for these men who were imprisoned on our behalf, for whom the wounds may be deep, invisible and unreachable, it may be that we can do little more, but certainly no less, than open our arms and our hearts, and bid them WELCOME... WELCOME...HOME

Finally, two years later, the terrible war would finally end:

Commentary—April 29, 1975

For me, as for many, I presume our costly, questionable involvement in Viet Nam is recalled in bits and pieces, like the shifting fragments of colored glass in a child's kaleidoscope.

At first, the pieces all fit together, illuminated by the optimism of Presidents' and Generals' who would call it "a light at the end of the tunnel."

But, as months became years—as U.S. advisors became full-scale invaders—shadows began to fall upon the screen of the Viet Nam kaleidoscope.

The pieces no longer fit together in a neat, predictable fashion.

The snapshots of war, at first so ordered and noble, were now shocking and grotesque: green hillsides incinerated by napalm, the sights of a naked girl screaming down a highway, the specter of a Vietnamese official summarily blowing out the brains of a Viet Cong suspect.

And the suppressed details of a young Army lieutenant leading his platoon at a place called My Lai.

And, with such televised sights came new sounds:

"Hell no...I won't go."

"Hey, hey, LBJ. How many babies did you kill today?"

The violence of the battlefield ultimately was mirrored in America's cities and campuses.

The images of this kaleidoscope became a national Rorschach test...and the prognosis was grave.

Still, there was a "light at the end of the tunnel": Paris, peace talks, withdrawal, and homecoming.

But, it, too, would flicker: invasion, collapse, refugees, and evacuation.

And, now, finally, the kaleidoscope is dark. The images frozen. No more "light at the end of the tunnel." For, thank God...no more tunnel!

Joel Daly

Scott *Kelly* *Doug*

Suez Canal – 1973

The Daly News

Mayor Richard J. Daley

Moscow – 1989

Joel Daly

Joel Daly arrived at WBKB in 1967 as anchor of *NewsNight*, the station's weeknight newscast. He was paired with former WBBM-TV veteran Fahey Flynn in 1968 on the *Flynn-Daly News*. Although they were not the first news team in Chicago, Flynn and Daly made broadcast history when they were instructed by station manager Richard O'Leary to occasionally break from the scripts and offer some personal asides. The chemistry between the veteran newsman and the rising young reporter was undeniable, and the resultant "happy talk" changed the face of local news forever. The team was together until Flynn's untimely death in 1983, with Daly continuing at WLS-TV until his retirement in 2005. In addition to his broadcast accomplishments, which include induction into the Chicago Journalism Hall of Fame and the NATAS Silver Circle as well as earning five Emmy awards, Daly is also a practicing trial lawyer, a stage actor, and even finds time to yodel in a country band. (MBC.)

Courtesy – Museum of Broadcast Communication

Chapter 9

"Come Fly With Me...Come Fly With Me..."

All this time, while I worked nights, Sue was at home raising the kids. It wasn't fair and it wasn't always fun. But she was a saint. The boys, Doug and Scott, were hellions, who ultimately got into the '70's drug scene. We sent Doug to a Military School where the discipline paid off. Scott was in a number of rehab institutions where he finally found some peace in his music. He became a marvelous guitar and bass player. But neither boy could ever escape the curse.

Kelly was "Daddy's Girl," the picked-upon sibling who persevered. These were my thoughts on her first day of school:

Commentary—September 2, 1969

I lost my little girl today. She went off to school for the first time, proudly following her older brothers up the ladder that leads to our "big world."

It was just the first day and the first step is an easy one. But it was the first time the house was empty, the home where she had been queen.

Now, she had abdicated that position and put aside her father's throne for some teacher's desk.

She gave me one final look, one final encouraging wave, as if to say: "I've got to learn, like you, the wonders of books, the beauty of people, the lessons of history, and the faith of the future."

She will know soon enough that her world, like ours, will probably include tears, tragedy and sorrow. Hopefully, she will learn that for every enemy there's a friend, for every scoundrel there's a hero, and that "bullies" are the easiest people to defeat.

It was just the first day of so many days. It's just the first tiny step in a thousand miles of experience. But she was the last to leave, and, so, somewhat selfishly and with regret, I said goodbye to my little girl who's not so little any more.

Growing up was so much harder than when I was a boy. And it wasn't easy being the offspring of a "celebrity." Later, I mused about the role of "fatherhood:"

Commentary—June 19, 1970

This was a day when they sold funny cards and little packages: pipes and ties and shaving lotion. Seldom any last minute shopping for Father's Day, for only a father, it seems, shops at the last minute.

A father is a funny fellow and why not? No one gives him much credit for becoming a father. Few give him much advice on being a father. He acts tough and talks gruff, but is really very gentle and often a little scared. A father's discipline is usually reserved for his son the one, everyone says, "looks and acts just like him." A father saves his fondest bewilderment for his little girl, the one, as they say: "he will someday give away to a man who isn't nearly good enough, so they can have grandchildren who are smarter than anyone's."

A father is a funny fellow, a little boy grown up—concerned now, because war is no longer a game and a gun is no longer a toy. The world looks so different through the eyes of a father.

A father makes bets with an insurance company, knowing he will lose, but he keeps betting and working, and privately praying, for that's what fathers are supposed to do. But, fathers aren't supposed to cry or get sentimental, so they swallow hard and feign surprise when confronted with funny cards and little packages. "Oh, it's Father's Day!" What else can he say?

A father is an awfully funny fellow.

One of my childhood dreams was to learn how to fly. Many days, as a kid, I would ride my bike to Felts Field, outside of Spokane, and watch the planes take off and land. That was why leaving Air Force ROTC was such a tough decision. In 1970, I did a story on a glider club in the western suburbs. I got a ride and I was hooked. I started taking lessons. But one didn't get much flight time sniffing the weak thermals rising from the cornfields so I graduated to little planes with real engines.

Like my days at Yale, and later in law school, I put my mind to a rigorous curriculum. I learned everything I could about flight dynamics, navigation, and the weather. After receiving a private license, I went on—with help from my untapped GI benefits—to learn instrument and multi-engine flying, Ultimately, I qualified as a flight instructor.

I became Channel 7's aviation expert and reported on all kinds of planes and pilots. On one occasion, I even tried "wing-walking". It was at the airport of Lewis University in Romeoville. I was there to promote a "fly-in" that weekend. Gene Littlefield was a resident stunt pilot who regularly flew his vintage bi-plane, in air shows, with a pretty girl on the wing. I mention the "pretty girl" because she was 5-foot-two, a full foot shorter than me. So, I had to crouch, against the pylon, throughout the flight to withstand the head winds. That was uncomfortable enough. But, the worse part of the trip was take-off and landing in a cloud of "bugs", stirred up by the propeller. A pair of goggles protected my eyes, but the little critters smashed, unimpeded against my teeth!

Commentary—March 29, 1977

It wasn't much of an incident, really: An old cargo plane veered off a runway at O'Hare and was destroyed. The two crewmen escaped with burns.

In the wake of the Canary Island tragedy, the story barely rated a mention, except in connection with the weather.

"A twin-engine plane," said most experts, "propeller-driven." Only parenthetically was it identified as a DC-3.

A DC-3. It's not that I'm ancient. But, I suddenly realized an entire generation has grown up on big, silver airplanes that push their way through the air instead of grabbing for it with powerful propellers.

The airplane destroyed last night at O'Hare was more than a "twin-engine, propeller-driven relic." It was one of the greatest airplanes ever built!

The DC-3 literally rescued our floundering airline industry, back in the '30's. By the time production ended in 1945, the DC-3 probably represented nearly half the planes in the sky. It was still toting guns during Viet Nam.

Military pilots lovingly called it the *gooney bird*. One of them wrote: "It rattled, it protested, it leaked oil, it ran hot, it ran cold, and it ran rough. It staggered along on hot days, and scared you half to death. Its wings flexed and twisted in a horrifying manner. It sank back to earth with a great sigh of relief. But, it flew and flew and flew. Honest faithful and magnificent machine that it was."

Forty years later, some 3,000 are still in the air. The DC-3 is half as old as aviation itself. And, more than any other airplane, responsible for its growth.

That's why I felt the old gooney that burned last night deserved a better obituary. After all those years and all those hours, in all that weather, fate had to sneak up on her—on the ground—when she wasn't looking.

I flew whatever and whenever I could. During a series of on-scene reports with the Air Force, I got to take the controls of a U-2 spy plane 15 miles over the San Francisco Bay area. From that altitude, I could see three states and note the curvature of the earth. I also had a seat in a fighter jet engaged in a mock dogfight over the Nevada desert. My logbook had some interesting entries:

In 1978, while attending the Oshkosh Flight Convention, I saw the plane of my dreams: a fully-aerobatic, multi-colored bi-plane—the Christen Eagle. It was a kit plane which one had to build. For the next two years, mostly on weekends, I put the plane together—with help from a young man who knew what he was doing! In 1980 I proudly showed it off at Oshkosh—only the seventh of its type built, at the time. Twenty years later and after many hours of thrilling flight time, I donated the plane to the Aviation Department of Lewis University, so other young men could take it apart, put it back together, and dream my dream.

Wing Walker

Christen Eagle

"Come Fly with Me"–Album Cover

Chapter 10

"Yodel-Lay-Hee-Hoo..."

In the early days, before the network usurped the early morning and late nighttime periods, WLS mounted local productions. In 1973, I was asked to guest-host the late night talk show—any subject I wanted. I decided to do a program on "country music"—something I had learned to love from my days on the ranch in Montana. I invited a popular Western Trio—"The Sundowners"—to perform. I had met the guys—Don Walls, Bob Boyd, and Curt Delaney—on one of my earliest visits to the "Bar-Double-R," then located in the basement of a building, next to the bus station, on Madison. I occasionally sat in and sang a song, or two.

The program caught the attention of an editor at the Chicago Tribune who asked me to write an article on the "country music scene" for the Tribune Magazine. It would be published during the annual Livestock Show. That gave me the whole summer to visit a number of country music clubs and take notes.

While listening to a group at the Lake 'N Park Inn, in southwest suburban Palos Hills, I was recognized and encouraged to "come up and tell a joke." I told the bandleader: "I don't tell jokes, but give me a *C* chord and I'll sing a little yodel." Which I did! That was the beginning of a most fulfilling career as an "entertainer." At first, I appeared as a "guest artist' with a number of local bands, but ultimately teamed up, full time, with the Sundowners. We worked together for nearly 30 years!

Joel Daly

One weekend in 1976, I was flying back from New York after my network news appearance—a perk I bartered from our local success—to emcee a big Country Music Concert at McCormick Place, featuring among others, Dolly Parton and the Oak Ridge Boys. On the plane, I wrote a poem called *A Hillbilly*, and read it to the audience:

A hillbilly is not just one who lives in the hills...
Who drinks from the stills or works in the mills.

A hillbilly is not just one whose neck is red...
Whose tail is lead, or is by a shotgun wed.

No, a hillbilly isn't just a mountaineer ready to feud.
A hillbilly isn't merely a person, it's an attitude!

A hillbilly loves people. He knows their joy and their grief...
And a hillbilly knows laughter is the key to relief.

Laughter and tears purge the heart of its weight...
Leaving no room for fear, mistrust or hate.

A hillbilly puts his feelings and life into song...
Of lonely nights, empty arms and love that's gone wrong.

It's real. It's honest. It's relevant and true...
A song about someone else that says something about you!

A hillbilly looks for the light, not the heat...
Of the type that's generated by a rock 'n roll beat.

So call me hillbilly. Make me part of that crowd.
At least I know when music is good and not just too loud.

And, if my poem sounds corny and just a little bit silly...
What the heck do you expect...I'm just a hillbilly!

The poem created something of a stir. Dolly asked if she could have a copy to read on her television show in Nashville. Columnist Bob Greene published it in the Tribune and hundreds wrote in for copies. Later in the year, I got a call from a record producer, in Nashville—Scotty Turner—asking me to "come on down and record it." What fun! We put a yodel on the "B" side. And Sue started selling T-shirts at my concerts.

Over the years, the Sundowners and I produced four "live-concert-albums." A single

I recorded, entitled *Rocky Mountain Oysters* was "number one" on the charts in Janesville, Wisconsin and peaked at "number four" in Ketchikan, Alaska!

Dolly Parton

wJJd
Chicago Country

WEEK OF   OCTOBER 25, 1976

1. You and Me — Tammy Wynette
2. The Games That Daddies Play — Conway Twitty
3. Peanuts and Diamonds — Bill Anderson
4. Among My Souvenirs — Marty Robbins
5. A Whole Lotta Things to Sing About — Charley Pride
6. *Cherokee Maiden — Merle Haggard
7. Somebody Somewhere — Loretta Lynn
8. Here's Some Love — Tanya Tucker
9. After the Storm — Wynn Stewart
10. *Her Name Is — George Jones
11. *9,999,999 Tears — Dickey Lee
12. Show Me a Man — T. G. Sheppard
13. Whiskey Talkin — Joe Stampley
14. Come On In — Sonny James
15. That Look in Her Eyes — Freddie Hart
16. Let's Put It Back Together Again — Jerry Lee Lewis
17. Living It Down — Freddy Fender
18. Can't You See — Waylon Jennings
19. Thinkin' of Rendezvous — Johnny Duncan
20. *Baby Boy — Mary Kay Place
21. I'm Gonna Love You — Dave & Sugar
22. Love Is Thin Ice — Barbara Mandrell
23. A Hillbilly — Joel Daly
24. That'll Be the Day — Linda Ronstadt
25. I Don't Want to Have to Marry You — Brown & Cornelius
26. Thank God I've Got You — Statler Brothers
27. Good Woman Blues — Mel Tillis
28. She Never Knew Me — Don Williams
29. Take My Breath Away — Margo Smith
30. Kiss and Say Goodbye — Billy Larkin

WJJD Music Line Requests

CHICAGO RADIO **wJJd**
Country Radio
1160 AM
104.3 FM Stereo

Ted Clark
afternoons

The Sundowners

THE SINGING ANCHORMAN

Frank Reynolds, Max Robinson, Bill Beutel, Joel Daly, Fahey Flynn and Fred Van Amburg. All are ABC anchormen. But only one of them has written a song about it. Joel Daly.

An award-winning newsman at WLS-TV in Chicago for 16 years, Daly has a passion for writing, singing and playing country music. He does it, he says, because "country music tells a story about people's everyday lives, their hopes, their fears, their loneliness and their happiness. When I have something to say I like to use my music. It's the perfect way to get a message across."

How does a song's story compare with a news story? Consider the lyrics from a Daly composition: "The critics all say that you gotta be straight, when reporting on war, violence, death and hate. But I always look for love in the land, Thank God I'm an Anchorman!"

Country music, with its origins in the South and Southwest, and reporting for WLS-TV News in urban Chicago, are two very different vocations. But Daly finds similarities. "The two are actually very much alike. Country music is not about kings and queens. It's about the working class people and about things we all go through just surviving. The stories I report every night on the news have the same elements. On stage as a singer, or on television as an anchorman, I'm communicating about what happens in all of our lives."

Daly's musical career began hundreds of miles away from the Windy City. "I grew up in Montana and started playing trumpet in the first grade," he says. "I've been in music virtually all my life." Once he discovered that playing an instrument was not his strong suit, he decided to develop a different talent – singing.

However, it wasn't until he attended Yale University that Daly began thinking seriously about singing as an avocation. "I sang with one of Yale's college singing groups," he says, "not because I was great at harmony, but because I could yodel, something I learned while working on a ranch in Montana. That was my introduction to singing."

After Yale, Daly channeled his energies into his career as a journalist. But the Big Sky country and the music stayed in his heart. His job at WLS in Chicago began in 1967. So did his singing career with The Sundowners. By coincidence, or fate, he met them the very first night he was in the city.

"The Sundowners had been performing at a little country bar in the heart of the Loop for 26 years. It's a remarkably consistent record, and one unequalled in the music business," says Daly.

Together, Daly and The Sundowners have performed in many of the popular nightclubs in the Chicago area. They have opened for the biggest names in country music including Ronnie Milsap, The Statler Brothers, Mel Tillis and The Oak Ridge Boys. Yet, Daly prefers doing concerts. "It's really more interesting," he says. "In nightclubs we are often limited to doing a short, 20-25 minute show," he explains. "In concert we have the opportunity to feature everyone in the band. It's more interesting."

The Sundowners – a lead guitar, a rhythm guitar, piano, drums and a bass – can more often be seen headlining county fairs and festivals. At the annual Orville Redenbacher Festival in Valparaiso, Indiana, The Sundowners played to a crowd of about 50,000 country music fans. "It was sort of like entertaining to a country mini-Woodstock," says Daly.

"I really enjoy the reactions I get from a live audience," says Daly. "They hear songs they can identify with, and they're obviously enjoying themselves. I'm so pleased ABC has indulged my desire to perform in front of a live audience in addition to my job in front of the camera."

Daly enjoys a special relationship with his audience. Although his television audience is varied, his concert audience is more specialized. To express how he feels about his concert audience, Daly wrote and recorded a song called "Hillbilly." It hit the radio charts and even reached number four in Ketchikan, Alaska. "The song answered the criticism of people who put down country music lovers. A lot of people feel the way I do; I'm proud to be a 'hillbilly,'" says Daly.

On stage, The Sundowners are clad in traditional western shirts and faded jeans. Daly's lively western outfit, complete with feathered cowboy hat, is a far cry from the conservative suits he wears on *Eyewitness News*. But his face is instantly recognizable as is his clear voice. "People often come a first time out of curiosity, and the second time they want to hear us sing," says Daly.

Dressed for the occasion, the band begins with one of Daly's original compositions, such as "The Difference in Me." It has become Daly's trademark because of his yodeling. Then the pace changes to an upbeat medley of popular songs – "fun kind of music," describes Daly. A concert closes with renditions of classical country music by such great artists as Hank Williams, Bob Wills and Eddy Arnold. Daly enjoys these songs the most. "My personal feeling is that most country groups try to imitate current hit records. There is some appeal in that, but it is usually derivative. I like to play the songs that are timeless and say something and have meaning for people," explains Daly.

Concerts sometimes bring with them unusual experiences. Once, during an outdoor concert, The Sundowners played "I Love You Truly" for a couple getting married in a hot-air balloon. Halfway through the song, Daly noticed that the balloon was being inflated, right between the bandstand and the audience! "We persevered," says Daly, "and went on with the rest of the show, playing to a large, hot-air balloon."

Does Daly's active avocation hurt his image or credibility on the news? He doesn't think so. "When I get out there with these people, the reaction usually is, 'Gee, you're a real human being, just like us.' When I'm on television, I'm distanced more. When I'm performing, I feel three dimensional. It enhances my credibility. I enjoy doing the news and I have a good time singing. That's the main thing. Aside from that, it's the best public relations I can do!"

Chapter 11

"The Times They Are A-Changin'"

Commentary—January 3, 1974

My mind, I must confess, sometimes works in strange ways, but I was fascinated by the coincidence that folk-singer Bob Dylan happened to resurface in Chicago on the very same day indictments were dropped against the so-called "Weatherman" group, which took its name from a Bob Dylan lyric: "You don't need a weatherman to know which way the wind blows."

In the early 60's, Bob Dylan was an angry, introspective young man, who said of himself: "I accept chaos. I am not sure whether it accepts me…" His songs were full of hurt and protest, reflecting the frustrations of his generation, cynical young people, some of whom ultimately reacted in senseless violence in what became known, four years ago, here in Chicago, as the "Days of Rage."

But to paraphrase Dylan, you don't need a weatherman to know the wind is blowing a different way today.

Bernadine Dohrn, a ringleader of the group, and one of the few women ever to make the F.B.I.'s "ten most wanted list," was quietly dropped recently and no one seemed to care.[1]

Today, the indictments were thrown out, with little protest, and indeed, the government with its embarrassing record of unauthorized wiretapping, comes off as the villain. The "Days of Rage" are over.

And, if we needed any further evidence, here comes Bob Dylan, no longer the angry young man, but at 32, the president of his own record company, who launched his tour, not as a protest, but as a way to make millions of dollars.

As he, himself, once said: "The times, they are a-changin'."

The times were "a-changin'" for me, as well.

The ratings were slipping. A decade of news-

---

[1] Bernadine Dohrn is now a Clinical Professor of Law and immediate past director/funder of the Children and Family Justice Center at Northwestern University. She is married to William Ayers, former leader of the "Weatherman."

dominance was ending. There were new general managers, and news directors. Consultant Frank Magid began tinkering with the format: shorter stories, less political news, more "reporter-involvement." In 1978, the Station decided to cut out the daily commentaries. This was the last one I contributed on a regular basis:

Commentary—January 27, 1978

Georgie Jessel once said of show business: "Nothing is so permanent as change." And that certainly includes television!

This is my last regularly scheduled commentary on this program.

It is the judgment of management that they are anachronistic, time-consuming and action-stopping; that they do not enhance the tempo of a contemporary news program, or properly utilize the new electronic tools of the trade.

Furthermore, it is their opinion that devoting myself to preparing a daily commentary dissipates energy and experience that might better serve the program in other ways.

So be it?

Ten years, more than 3,000 commentaries. Never sued, never censored. It's a record of which I am proud.

Never intended to preach or provoke or hurt, the nightly essays into which I poured so much pride and effort were conceived simply to make you think and occasionally to make you smile.

Never a critical success, they didn't fit the critic's concept of biting controversy. Too much heart and not enough hardness I fear. But during the incredible decade just passed, they provided a forum for fact and opinion that would otherwise have been ignored.

I have a bookshelf of awards, including three Emmys. The last of which I am most proud: an award for "Best Television Writing."

In a medium where so often the picture ignores perspective, and motion, becomes meaning, it was a great satisfaction to harvest the riches of language, to write a little poetry, to quote a little Shakespeare. Or e.e. cummings who said: "The reward in a job well done is having done it." I have done it, and I am richly rewarded.

And, if it's true, "nothing is so permanent as change," nothing can change the permanency of the experiences we shared the past 10 years.

But now I look forward to new opportunities—new challenges and projects—that will still in some way say, "I'm Joel Daly."

Now, years later, when I'm recognized, many people still comment on the Commentaries. Usually, they remember something I said that I don't even recall. But, one thing virtually everyone remembers is "Mr. Food." Let me explain.

I was a "news purist", resisting, usually unsuccessfully, efforts by management and their mercenary "consultants" to dilute the product with non-news "features". And, so to my great dismay, I returned from a vacation, one August afternoon, and found something called "Mr. Food" on the 4:00 News menu. "Mr. Food", I scoffed. "What is that?"

"It's a feature we started while you were gone: a daily, quick-fix recipe presented by a guy with a chef's hat, full facial hair and an oozy sign-off: "OOooo it's SOooo GOOood"! "Mr. Food". "His real name is Art Ginsburg."

It would be an understatement to say, I was less than thrilled. So, still sight-unseen, that evening I introduced the segment with an outrageously sarcastic "MISTER Food." I did the same thing for a week and decided enough was enough. I had made my point. (I think). Then viewers started calling and writing: "Are you being censored? What happened to MISTER Food?" They were turned on by my turn off. It became obligatory!

Then, the moment of truth: Art showed up for a "live-appearance". During the commercial, I sheepishly explained that I had been exaggerating his title, a little. Art looked at me, with a stern expression: "I know...(pause) <u>keep doing it.</u> That's all I hear wherever I go in Chicago and even at home in Florida!" He could have said: "OOooo it's SOOoo GOOood."

Eventually, Fahey and I were demoted from the 10:00 News. We were replaced by sportscaster-turned-anchorman, Tim Weigel, and Mary Ann Childers. It was subtly suggested that I should look elsewhere for work. Sue and I took a vacation trip to other towns: Denver, San Francisco, San Diego, and Phoenix. We decided we wanted to stay in Chicago and we did. We were true *Midwesterners*—a special "breed" I had described several times:

Commentary—December 12, 1972

Midwesterners, I've always felt, are a distinctive breed of people: friendly, hardy, and humorous.

Excepting swimming and tennis, most major sports seem to be dominated by athletes from the Midwest. Certainly, the arts, architecture, and industry have been vitalized by corn-belt progeny.

Even when you travel elsewhere, it seems, the people who keep things going, who run the hotel, or pump the gas, are transplanted Midwesterners.

Why is this? What makes the Midwesterner so unusual?

Well, I have a theory...it's the weather: the short wet springs, the long hot summers, the precious falls and the bitter winters.

Have you ever seen steel tempered?

First it's heated until its red-hot, and then plunged into cold water. This process rearranges the molecules and makes it stronger and more durable than ordinary steel. I suspect extreme weather may have a similar effect on Midwesterners.

How else could a person survive a God-awful day like this one? Sitting in a stalled El-train requires patience. Pushing a neighbor out of the slush engenders friendliness. And squinting at life through a smeary windshield requires a mind-saving sense of humor.

My theory may be a bit self-serving, as it suggests those of us in the Midwest are "something special." But, it made sense to me as I waited for the tow-truck today. I mean there must be some reason why we put up with this, year after year!

During the summer of 1983, while Sue and I were vacationing at our vacation home in Coeur d' Alene, Idaho, we received word that Fahey had died. I flew back to deliver a eulogy at his funeral:

>Mary has asked me to say a few words about Fahey, our friend whom we miss and mourn. What I can say, any of you could say: all of you who knew and loved this kind gentle man.

'Time'...there's just not enough time.

Fahey learned the presence and pressures of time early in life. The son of a railroad man with the most accurate watch in Escanaba, Michigan. It was there where summer's heat and winters icy cold combined to temper the soft dreams of a child into the resolute steel of a man.

'Time'...both a friend and yet a foe. The children grew so fast, nurtured by their father's warmth and patience and understanding. Their father...Fahey Flynn...a public figure who provided them a shelter of privacy and gave them a space to grow.

"Give them room," he would caution me, when we talked of our children. "Hold them, help them, but don't drive them away. There's not enough time!"

Fahey found time to build bridges across the gap of generations, always willing to listen, to learn and grow with them. In the lateness of his life, a life of much adulation, achievement, great awards, Fahey found his greatest reward: a trip to Water Tower, the zoo or some other magical place with his grandchildren.

But **'time'**...There just wasn't enough time.

And it was always that way. In a sometimes cold, cruel uncertain profession, the scramble of those early days...7 days a week, on the go...on the clock, from one station to another...from the ballpark to the studio... from the Aragon Ballroom on Saturday night, to the newsroom on a Sunday morning.

So little **'time'**...so much stress, meeting the deadlines, providing the bridge was down.

And yet there was always time for a quiet dinner and quiet words. Fahey found the time. He made the time. Long before Flynn-Daly, Fahey and Mary were the original team in this town. And even after such a long time, after nearly 50 years of broadcasting, Mary was still his biggest fan, his kindest critic.

'Time'...only so much time...and Fahey was a competitor. He wanted to win, and win he did. But, never at the expense of someone else...never with an unkind act...an unfair advantage.

In our peculiar world of *prima donnas*, Fahey Flynn was a *prima persona*, one of a kind. A man of tact, a man of sensitivity, for whom rank had no particular privilege.

My **'time'** became part of his **'time'**. More than 15 years we worked side by side. with never an unkind word. We never left the studio with any misgivings or unresolved grievances.

That's a remarkable record for any relationship. But, we're talking about **'time'**. A tense, turbulent time. There was death in the jungles far away...demonstrations...

disruptions in the streets at home. Tears and tear gas, such terrible times. Yet, side by side we bottled the emotion. Never an argument, yet another testimony to Fahey's great sense of respect for all things...all people... any idea, large or small.

Fahey had very strong feelings, deeply held political and philosophical convictions. But he never let them show "on the air..." During this time of great change and great debate, Fahey was steadfast...his eyebrows as straight as his familiar bow tie.

Fahey was the original, quintessential anchorman. Unmoved, unemotional, a man whom people trusted to tell them the truth... without endorsement or embellishment.

Fahey Flynn fought the odds of time in a very tough business in a very tough town. And his tenure, all that **'time'** as a broadcaster and newsman belie the unfortunate myths which cloud our profession: that it is cosmetic...that it is shallow... that it is "slick and superficial." For Fahey, the most successful of all, was none of these.

On the contrary, what you saw was what you got...what he was—a decent, caring human being.

If we just had more **'time'**. Any of you could have said any of this. Of Fahey's qualities, so obvious and so visible every night at 6:00 and 10:00. I am simply privileged to speak today on your behalf.

But, may I add, most of you saw Fahey from the front, that wide Irish smile, that white hair reflecting the studio lights. I saw him from the side, and from that angle, I could see the effects of **'time'**. I could watch the lines of concern deepen in his brow... year after year.

Concern for the direction and application of the medium he so loved. Concern that old standards, which he helped pioneer, were getting lost in the new technology. Concern that youth had replaced experience.

From my place at his side, I could see the pain he would never let you see, following that terrible fall, that would have retired a less courageous man. But, Fahey, tempered by the Midwest weather and nurtured by Midwest people, was a survivor, who would not give up. He would not retire!

Even in these final weeks, in his final struggle to restore a body that could no longer withstand the punishment of **'time'**, he was there, on the job...ready to work...to serve his community...to support his colleagues.

For many years, at the beginning and end of our news programs, the camera would show the two of us talking. You couldn't tell what we were saying to each other. That, naturally, aroused a lot of curiosity. People would invariably ask me; "What do you and Fahey talk about every night?"

Usually, I'd just smile and remain non-committal, as if it were some kind of secret. We were two men bound in **'time'**—victims of the unrelenting clock. And, we talked about living and dying...of where we had been...and where we were going...if we only had **'time'**.

And, those conversations would often last long after the studio lights went out. We would sit there in the darkness, as if unwilling to let go. It was the one **'time'**, we had **'time'**. Those were the moments, I will most remember. That rich voice rolling out of the darkness, spinning a tale from the past...or posing a question of the future—often funny, sometimes sad—intimate words that could be said and shared without the presence of the clock...without the witness of the world.

But now **'time'** has run out!

No more deadlines, my dear friend...no more rush.

No more stories to send...no more fuss.

So rest in peace, dear friend...and be to heaven bound.

We'll follow for **'time'** must end...Just pray the bridge is down!

Chapter 12

"Res ipsa loquitur..."

The Weigel-Childers experiment ended in failure. I was put back on the 10:00 News with *anchors du jour*. But, I knew it was temporary. The word was that John Drury, an old colleague, was coming back to Channel 7, at the end of his contract with WGN, to anchor the late news. Of course, it was true. He returned and I was assigned to an early afternoon program, which I wrongfully dubbed "News for Shut-ins."

Dennis Swanson, the then-general manager, knew I was unhappy. He took me to lunch, and proposed to extend my contract, which then had a year left. I told him "no"—I would take my chances somewhere else. "What can I offer to change your mind?", he asked. What a great opportunity! I suggested all kinds of perks, but he balked at giving me a parking space in the company garage. What else could I extort? I flashed on my consideration of graduate opportunities when at Yale, and my experience during the Sheppard trial, and I announced, emphatically: "And, I'm going to go to law school, at night, so you'll have to cut me some slack." I thought that would be the deal-breaker! Dennis paused and pondered: "Anything else," he asked? That night, I announced to Sue that I was going to law school. I was approaching my 50th birthday!

I did well on the LSAT exam and had several choices. I chose Chicago Kent College of Law, in the old building at Adams and Wacker, primarily because it was within a brisk walk, following the 4:00 News. It was great being back in school. And, the company paid my tuition.

My first night of class, the Contracts Professor, Randy Barnett, quoted the familiar opening to Rod Serling's "Twilight Zone".

Then he added his own version:

> You unlock this door with the key of imagination. Beyond it is another dimension—a dimension of sound, a dimension of sight, a dimension of mind. You're moving into a land of both shadow and substance, of things and ideas. You've just crossed over into—LAW SCHOOL.

I sat in the front row and wrote that down, as if it would be on a final exam. I always took copious notes. Then I received a *C* on a legal writing paper. What? Me? A professional writer, an Emmy winner! It was just part of the "weeding out" process that all first year law students must endure. Actually, for "night students" it went on for four years, including two summers.

During my second year, I participated on a Moot Court Team that won the regional competition and went on to New York for the finals. I began to think I would enjoy being a lawyer! Through it all Sue was supportive and resilient. She did all the driving, on weekends, to our vacation home in Southern Wisconsin, so I could read. My life became very structured.

My fourth and final year, I was a member of the Trial Team that won the National Competition, held in Dallas. It was the first time for the school and we were proudly praised at graduation in 1988. Two years later, another proud event! My daughter, Kelly, walked across the same stage and I put on her "hood" signifying she was also a *Doctor of Jurisprudence*. She accepted her diploma with my toddling granddaughter, Katelyn, walking beside her.

Because of my trial experience I was invited to join Corboy & Demetrio, a prestigious personal injury firm, in Chicago, as a part-time associate. Phil Corboy explained that a good trial lawyer must have, what he called, the "Four C's:"

competency, credibility, charisma and caring. The same qualities as a successful anchorman. The problem is neither is a "part-time job." After a year, I left the firm to go out on my own.

At about the same time I entered law school, I was paired with Linda Yu, as co-anchors on the 4:00 pm News. She was very supportive and we became close friends. Our partnership would last for 21 years, and the 4:00 News was a solid number one! Forget my sarcasm about "News for Shut-ins."

One afternoon while performing a concert in Oak Lawn, a woman asked me "Where's Linda?" "On vacation." "Where?" "I don't know." "Why not. Aren't you her father?"

Linda loved the story. I concocted a tale of how I found her, as an infant, in rushes along the Yalu River while I was in Korea and raised her. With Fahey, it was "father-son." With Linda, it was "father-daughter." Despite the fact our ages are about a decade apart.

My law school experience actually made me a better reporter, a more insightful interrogator. I produced a weekly legal affairs segment called "Law Review" that won a number of awards and helped me get more acquainted with the local legal community.

Ultimately, I joined forces with Burt Joseph, a premier First Amendment lawyer, who taught a seminar while I was in law school. We tried several cases together. But, the most unusual—if not the most fun—was the case of Themis Klotz. Themis was the divorced wife of a Northwestern Professor, a very bright woman, in her own right. But, she was a little eccentric!

The tony Village of Glencoe brought action against her for a "Peace Park" she had constructed in front of her house. The "Park" consisted, among other things, of an old tire, swinging from a tree, scribbled with graffiti, a water heater that represented a rocket, and plastic pots, hanging from a bush, that symbolized helmets of the young men, from the neighborhood who died in Viet Nam. But the *piece d'resistance* was her old station wagon, covered with peace stickers, parked in the driveway that she had covered with 40 tons of sand. She was sculpting a whale to represent conservation of the earth. The neighbors weren't thrilled, naturally, and the Village complained she had broken local ordinances.

Burt and I defended Themis on first amendment grounds: freedom of speech and artistic expression! We even called experts on the subject. The Jury didn't buy it, but we did negotiate a settlement, which allowed the Village to come on her property twice a month, if necessary, eight months of the year. Basically, we got her free lawn service for life!

An interesting thing occurred, incidentally, during the jury selection. The Judge explained the issues, identified the parties and the lawyers, and asked if any of the prospective jurors knew any of them. One man raised his hand and said, "I know Mr. Daly from television." "Would that, in any way, make you unable to listen to the testimony and fairly apply the law?" asked the Judge. "Oh," said the man, "I believe everything Mr. Daly says." "Excused!" The others caught on. We lost the whole venire and had to pick a new panel the next day. The "celebrity thing" became an issue in several of my cases. It worked both for me and against me!

One of the nice things about being a Chicago lawyer was the opportunity to perform in *Christmas Spirits*, the annual Bar show. I visited an audition, just after passing the bar exam. The director, Len Rubin, told Julian Frazin, the chief writer, to compose a solo for me. That was unheard of. It usually took many years of chorus work before one got to sing a solo. The "celebrity thing" again!

"What do you do?" Julie asked. "Well, I sing a little country, do a little yodeling," I answered. That night, he called to sing me the lyrics of a song he wrote to the tune of the *Lonely Goatherd*. I still remember the first verse:

> "Hello, my name is Joel Daly...Daly...
> Joel Daly...I'm the Daly who Brings you the
> News on Channel SEVEN; that's on Channel
> SEVEN, not on TWO.
>
> I'm here to interview Rich Daley...Daley...
> Richie Daley, not the Daly who Brings you the
> news on Channel SEVEN. That's on Channel
> SEVEN, not on TWO.

I performed in the Bar Show for the next 20 Christmases, playing a number of parts and singing a number of songs. I was "Fidel Castro" singing "O, Lonesome Me," with my harmonica secreted in a phony cigar. But my favorite song was the lament of a fully-costumed "Mad Cow" singing a parody of the Patsy Cline classic: *"Crazy...Everyone thinks, I am Crazy."*

In addition to trials, I did some appellate work and ultimately became a certified mediator. I was active in the bar associations and became a charter member of the Chicago Inn of Court—a collegial group of judges and trial lawyers who put on monthly programs. In 1990 the Inn accepted a British challenge to defend George Washington, on a charge of "treason." I was part of the trial team that went to London along with our key witnesses, Thomas Jefferson and Ben Franklin. George was acquitted!

I also played Clarence Darrow defending Buck Weaver and "Shoeless Joe Jackson," members of the 1919 "Black Sox," seeking reinstatement. Later I would portray the great Chicago lawyer in a one-man show on stage. But, my theatrical career began with a bit of chutzpah when I read that Wisdom Bridge Theater was preparing a production of *To Kill a Mockingbird*. I called the director and suggested I would make a marvelous Atticus Finch!

I auditioned and got the role, in no small part because of the "celebrity thing."

I sent a "Summons" to my friends:

SUMMONS

You are hereby summoned, to be a witness, at the County Court of Maycomb, Alabama where Atticus Finch *(as portrayed by Joel Daly)* will defend Tom Robinson in:

"TO KILL A MOCKINGBIRD"

Date of Appearance: January 27 - February 28, 1994

Location: **Wisdom Bridge Theatre
1559 West Howard Street
Chicago, Illinois 60626
(312) 743-6000**

It was a wonderful experience in a role I would reprise several times. Atticus has a lot to teach us about the dignity and decency of providing zealous advocacy: In a storm of public disapproval, Atticus tells his children: "There's been a lot of high talk around this town that I shouldn't do much about Tom Robinson (the black man falsely accused of raping a white woman). "But I'm going to defend that man."

"We'll be fighting our friends," he goes on to say. "But, remember this, no matter how bitter things get, they are still our friends, and this is still our home." "The Tom Robinson case must be pretty important," his young daughter, Scout, observes. Said Atticus: "One thing does not abide by majority rule, honey. It's your conscience."

In the final scene, after Boo Radley has rescued Jem from the murderous assault of Bob Ewell, Atticus is standing on his porch with Scout, who says, "Atticus, what Heck Tate (the Sheriff) said about Boo, about dragging him into the limelight—Heck is right!" "What do you mean?" asks Atticus. "I mean it'd be like shooting a mockingbird, wouldn't it? All those ideas we had about Boo Radley. But, Atticus, he's real nice!" Atticus smiles at his daughter and says, affectionately, "Most people are, Scout, when you finally see them."

The Chicago Reader, a notoriously vicious reviewer, said of my performance: "Joel Daly does not simply play Atticus Finch, He is Atticus Finch!"

Chicago Daily Law Bulletin

Since 1854

Volume 134, No. 60   Monday, March 28, 1988

Circuit Judge Warren Wolfson (right) with the members of IIT Chicago-Kent College of Law's winning trial advocacy team. The team members (from left to right), Joel Daly, Lauretta Higgins and Peter Roskam, won the 13th Annual National Trial Advocacy Competition last weekend in Dallas.

Chicago-Kent wins national trial advocacy competition

By a Law Bulletin staff writer

A student team from IIT Chicago-Kent College of Law became the first team from the midwest to win the 13th Annual Trial Advocacy Competition held last weekend in Dallas.

Team members are Joel Daly, an anchorman at Channel 7, Lauretta Higgins and Peter Roskam. They were coached by Cook County Circuit Judge Warren D. Wolfson.

"I am proud and happy," said Wolfson. "It's an incredible achievement ... and they will be a credit to the profession."

The team members, who are all night students, each received silver bowls and law books. Wolfson also received a silver bowl and will keep the traveling trophy for the year.

Roskam, a junior at Kent, was also named "best oral advocate." His prize consists of a trip to Toronto this August where he will address the annual meeting of the American College of Trial Lawyers, which co-sponsors the competition.

At that time, Kent will be given its prize of $5,000.

Other Kent faculty coaches for the winning team included Cook County Circuit Judge Thomas R. Fitzgerald of the Traffic Division and assistant Cook County state's attorney David A. Erickson.

Members of previous student teams also served as coaches. They were Karen L. Klaas of Phelan, Pope & John, Pat Morris of Johnson, Cusack & Bell and Ellen Mandeltort, an assistant state's attorney.

Continued on page 12
KENT

Kent
Continued from page 1

The winning mock trial was judged by Patrick E. Higginbotham of the 5th U.S. Circuit Court of Appeals and 12 lawyers from the American College of Trial Lawyers.

Wolfson said that the team spent more than 300 hours preparing for the national competition, which also included a team from Loyola University School of Law. Its team members are Scott Lane, Thomas Cushing and Kiplund Kolkmeier.

Kent and Loyola won the regional competition last month. The national competition began with 200 teams from law schools around the country. The 22 regional winners competed for the national honors in Dallas.

Wolfson said Kent teams have been selected as one of the two teams from this region for the last four years and five out of the last six in the national championships.

The contest, which began in 1975, is sponsored by the trial lawyers group, the American Bar Association Section on Litigation and its Young Lawyers Division. The finals were hosted last weekend by the Texas Young Lawyers Association at Southern Methodist University.

Peter Roskam, Hon. Warren Wolfson, Lauretta Higgins

Law School Graduation 1988

Kelly becomes a Lawyer 1990

Joel Daly

George Washington (back to camera), played by Bill Sommerfield, faces a court in London Thursday during a mock trial on charges of treason against the crown. The trial was taped for BBC Television.

Colonies rejoice: Washington cleared

By R.C. Longworth
Chicago Tribune

LONDON—George Washington will not hang at dawn.

A British-dominated court, deciding that the American colonies had the right to revolt, acquitted Washington Thursday night of charges of treason, gave him back his sword and sent him home.

It was a mock trial in the oak-paneled panoply of London's Lincoln Inn, with British barristers trying to prove Washington was a traitor to the crown, and a mostly Chicago-based team of defense lawyers out to save his neck and justify the American Revolution.

The judges—two British and one American—were real. So were the lawyers. George Washington and his two witnesses, Benjamin Franklin and Thomas Jefferson, were played by three Philadelphia-based actors who portray them for a living. The only prosecution witness, the prime minister of the era, Lord North, was played with gusto by a British professor of American history.

It was a mixture of old and new, trial and drama, reality and make-believe. But behind it was the issue of the right of a people to revolt against oppression. In the end, this right prevailed.

The leading judge, Lord Bridge of Harlech, ruled that though "the facts were beyond dispute"—Washington indeed led a revolt—the king and parliament had forfeited the colonies' allegiance through laws that robbed them of their liberties.

The British side, long since resigned to the loss of the colonies, were relaxed and ironic, treating the trial as sport.

The leading British barrister, Sydney Kentridge, noted at one point that the Declaration of Independence was signed on July 4, "a date which there is no particular reason to remember or note."

"None of us will be upset if Mr. Washington is acquitted," Kentridge admitted privately.

The Americans, by contrast, were in deadly earnest, appalled that they might lose America's greatest hero to the hangman's noose. While Kentridge quipped, they fought like tigers.

"I'm not sure we could have gone home if we'd lost," one lawyer said.

The American team was led by Chicago lawyers Michael Coffield and James Figliulo, aided by WLS-Ch. 7 anchor and lawyer Joel Daly and three New Jersey attorneys. The trial was born when Coffield and Figliulo accepted a challenge from a British judge in Washington last summer.

The decision by the British Broadcasting Corp. to televise the trial raised costs and tensions. Suddenly, the Americans were fighting for their national honor.

The pretense was that Washington had returned voluntarily to London in 1779 to answer the charge of treason. But the modern world kept intervening.

The British wore wigs, "Washington" wore his colonial uniform and his lawyers wore their business suits. Sniffer dogs checked the hall for bombs—Bridge once sentenced six alleged IRA terrorists to prison.

In 1779, Washington probably would have been hanged forthwith. In 1990, he was allowed to testify for himself.

Kentridge scored points off Jefferson's ownership of slaves. Lord North battered the defense with the combination of arrogance and upper-class accent that often cows Americans. He argued that taxes imposed on the colonies were necessary to pay Britain's bills there, "even thought I know Americans may have different attitudes toward borrowing and borrowing and borrowing."

Kentridge slipped in references to Britain's unpopular poll tax and asked Washington to look ahead "four-score years" to the possibility that the U.S. itself might use force to quell a rebellion.

"Sir, I am neither a seer nor a political theorist," Washington replied, while the judge told Kentridge, "You'll be talking next about flying to the moon."

But it was Coffield who drew the sharpest historical parallel when he said that, if Washington's ideals prevail, "a century or two from now, free Americans and free Englishmen may be required to draw a line in the sand for freedom."

In the end, the prosecution asked only that Washington be found guilty but freed and sent home to help the colonies "consider their position." The Americans rejected the deal and the judges, after 10 minutes, ruled "not guilty."

"Hello...My name is Joel Daly"

"O Lonesome Me"

THE NATIONAL LAW JOURNAL   Monday, March 21, 1994

HIS IDOL: Chicago attorney Joel Daly, standing, plays his hero, Atticus Finch, in a production of 'To Kill a Mockingbird.'

Roger Lewin/Jennifer Girard Studio

Lawyer Becomes His Own Hero

STEP ASIDE, Gregory Peck; there's a new Atticus Finch in Macomb, Ala. Joel Daly, Chicago television news anchor, lawyer, pilot and country and western singer has added live stage drama to his entertainment repertoire, just ending a run as the legendary Southern lawyer in "To Kill a Mockingbird," which is playing through April 3 at Chicago's Wisdom Bridge Theater.

Mr. Daly "doesn't play Atticus Finch; he is Atticus Finch," said a review in the Chicago Reader.

"I became my hero," says Mr. Daly, who co-anchors the 4 p.m. news on Chicago's WLS-TV and is of counsel at Barsey, Joseph & Lichtenstein. "I got to be the person that really motivated me later in my life to be a trial lawyer, to try do some good for my fellow man and woman."

Mr. Daly's January-through-February performance in the adaptation of Harper Lee's 1960 novel wasn't the first time he was cast in the role of his hero: In 1992, he won the first Atticus Finch Award from Chicago Volunteer Lawyers Service for publicizing its pro bono efforts.

After a show in late February, Mr. Daly and local defense lawyer Edward Genson discussed Finch's ethics before a group of law students from the Illinois Institute of Technology, Chicago-Kent College of Law. Mr. Daly praised the Depression-era lawyer's court-appointed defense of a black man accused of raping a white woman, refuting some claims that Finch didn't do enough to fight racial prejudice.

Mr. Daly's only previous stage experience has been participating for the past six years in the Chicago Bar Association's annual Christmas Spirits revue, in which he displays his accomplished yodeling in a variety of skits. He also is lead singer for The Sundowners, a country band that just recorded its second album.

"I can't deny that I have the bug," he says.

— *Randall Samborn*

Chapter 13

"September Song..."

"And, the days dwindle down, when you reach September..."

Like September, I could still feel the heat of summer but sense the beginning of Fall. Doug was married. He and Alicia gave us a second granddaughter—Madison. Kate was getting ready for college. My sister, Pat, was a nationally-recognized teacher in Des Moines. My stalwart Sue had endured some 30 different surgeries but carried on.

My final decade with Channel 7 was full of rewards and reminiscence. I was inducted into the Chicago Journalism Hall of Fame, as a "living legend." I stressed the word "living" in my response. I was accepted into the "Silver Circle" as a broadcaster who served the Chicago area, with distinction for 25 years or more. Later, I would receive the first-ever "Pioneer Award" from the Illinois Association of Broadcasters. Fahey had warned me that when you start receiving awards for what you've done, you're done!

In June of 2005, I reluctantly agreed to "retire." The station staged a magnificent send-off with a western-theme party at the Palmer House, complete with the "Shannon Rovers." There were proclamations from the Governor and the Mayor. I was honored by the Chicago City Council. Not bad for a kid from Montana!

Madison   Alicia   Doug

Madison

Family Reunion

Chapter 14

To Have Been...or not To Have Been

No, that's not Shakespeare! It's a paraphrase of Herodotus, history's first historian. When asked about "happiness," the Greek philosopher, said: "A man cannot know if he's truly happy until the end, when he can look back and see what he has done." By that measure, I can "look back" and say: "I am a happy man." I've done just about everything I wanted to do! I would still like to jump out of an airplane. There's always *Dancing with the Stars*. And, maybe, since I've learned how to work this word-processor, I'll try my hand at writing a novel.

After my long broadcast career, I taught, for several years, at the John Marshall Law School and Chicago Kent, although I "retired" my law license. I also worked as the Information Officer for the Federal District Court—a *pro bono* job that allowed me to see my old law and media colleagues when we had a "heater" or high-profile trial.

After 56 years of marriage, Sue and I are growing old gracefully and lovingly. We watch our marvelous daughter reaching for a new rainbow, and our granddaughter, Kate, following in the Daly tradition of learning and doing and dreaming. While Madison tells everyone, she's going to go to Yale, like her grandfather.

When we moved to Chicago in 1967, I told my young wife—who wasn't all that keen on taking a young family into the unknown and unfamiliar—"Look, I've got a two-year contract. Even if it only lasts for two years, Chicago will look good on my *resume*."

Incredibly since that time, I haven't had to write or distribute a resume. As someone said, "Success is getting what you want. Happiness is wanting what you get!"

By the way, I happened to visit that delicatessen where I had lunch on my first day of work. No one recognized me! Oh well... *tempus fugit.*

Kate *Kelly*

Doug

Emily Barr

Linda Yu

Kathy Brock

Alan Krashesky

Frank Mathie   Bob Petty

Also Available at Eckhartz Press

Behind the Camera by Chuck Quinzio

Records Truly is My Middle Name by John Records Landecker

Records Truly is My Middle Name, The Soundtrack (CD)

The Balding Handbook by David Stern

Cheeseland by Randy Richardson

The Living Wills by Rick Kaempfer and Brendan Sullivan

Down at the Golden Coin by Kim Strickland

Recalled to Life by Dan Burns

A Reluctant Immigrant by Felitzitas Sudendorf

ECKHARTZ PRESS

www.eckhartzpress.com